Cambridge Elements

Elements in Global Philosophy of Religion

edited by
Yujin Nagasawa
University of Oklahoma

SIKH ETHICS

Keshav Singh
The University of Alabama at Birmingham

CAMBRIDGE
UNIVERSITY PRESS

Shaftesbury Road, Cambridge CB2 8EA, United Kingdom

One Liberty Plaza, 20th Floor, New York, NY 10006, USA

477 Williamstown Road, Port Melbourne, VIC 3207, Australia

314–321, 3rd Floor, Plot 3, Splendor Forum, Jasola District Centre,
New Delhi – 110025, India

Cambridge University Press is part of Cambridge University Press & Assessment,
a department of the University of Cambridge.

We share the University's mission to contribute to society through the pursuit of
education, learning and research at the highest international levels of excellence.

www.cambridge.org
Information on this title: www.cambridge.org/9781009452304

DOI: 10.1017/9781009452311

First published 2026

A catalogue record for this publication is available from the British Library

*A Cataloging-in-Publication data record for this Element is available from the
Library of Congress*

ISBN 978-1-009-45230-4 Hardback
ISBN 978-1-009-45229-8 Paperback
ISSN 2976-5749 (online)
ISSN 2976-5730 (print)

Sikh Ethics

Elements in Global Philosophy of Religion

DOI: 10.1017/9781009452311
First published online: April 2026

Keshav Singh
The University of Alabama at Birmingham

Author for correspondence: Keshav Singh, keshavsingh@uab.edu

Abstract: Like many other world religious and spiritual traditions, the Sikh tradition is philosophically rich. However, its contributions have been wholly unrepresented in Western analytic philosophy. The goal of this Element is to present a central aspect of Sikh philosophy, its ethics, by using the tools and methods of analytic philosophy to reconstruct it in a form that is understandable to Western audiences, while still accurately capturing its unique and autochthonous features. On the interpretation of Sikh ethics this Element presents, the Sikh ethical theory understands ethics in terms of truthful living – in particular, living in a way that is true to the fundamental Oneness of all existence. Features of the Sikh ethical theory discussed include its account of vice and virtue, its account of right conduct, and the philosophical relationship between ethical theory and practice. This title is also available as Open Access on Cambridge Core.

Keywords: Sikh philosophy, Sikhism, truthful living, Oneness, non-Western philosophy

ISBNs: 9781009452304 (HB), 9781009452298 (PB), 9781009452311 (OC)
ISSNs: 2976-5749 (online), 2976-5730 (print)

Contents

Introduction

Like many other world religious and spiritual traditions, the Sikh tradition is philosophically rich. The primary Sikh scripture, Sri Guru Granth Sahib, contains a comprehensive philosophical system, with an integrated metaphysics, epistemology, philosophy of mind, and ethics. My focus in this work is on the ethics, though it is also necessary to say some things about the other aspects of Sikh philosophy in the process. It is meant for a variety of audiences: Western philosophers looking to better understand other traditions, Sikhs interested in an academic philosophical approach to understanding their own tradition, and anyone else intrigued by Sikh thought. On the interpretation I present, the Sikh ethical theory is an ethic of truthful living – living in a way that is true to the fundamental Oneness of all existence.

Despite containing a comprehensive philosophical system, Sikh philosophy has received almost no attention in Western analytic philosophy. This remains so even amid increasing engagement with other non-Western traditions. Though analytic philosophy is still predominantly a Western, Anglophone tradition in its demographics and practice, it aims to be defined not by its parochial intellectual history but by a methodology that focuses on clear and precise arguments and definitions of terms. In recent years, this analytic methodology has increasingly been used to draw out systematic philosophical theories from a variety of traditions. There is now significant work in analytic philosophy on a variety of non-Western traditions, including Islam, Buddhism, Confucianism, and Vedic traditions.

This diversification in the application of analytic methodology faces significant obstacles when it comes to Sikh philosophy. The primary text, Sri Guru Granth Sahib (hereafter SGGS), is not presented in a form that is familiar to Western audiences. It is comprised entirely of poetry written in an unfamiliar language, and its conceptual repertoire does not always correspond to that of Western thought, making accurate translation difficult.

As a result, non-Sikhs usually know very little about Sikh thought. Moreover, there are almost no Sikhs in philosophy departments in the West. As a result, there is virtually no one in philosophy departments in the West qualified to write about Sikh philosophy. Outside of philosophy departments, such as in the field of Sikh Studies, there have been attempts to engage philosophically with the Sikh tradition, but not using the analytic methodology.

Even in analytic philosophical texts that claim to broadly represent the philosophical history of South Asia, Sikh thought is completely absent. For example, Jonardon Ganeri is perhaps the preeminent philosopher writing about South Asian traditions. His 2011 book, *The Lost Age of Reason*, focuses on philosophical developments in South Asia from 1450–1700. The entirety of SGGS was written during this period, yet there is not even a single mention of the term "Sikh" in Ganeri's book, let alone any discussion of Sikh philosophy.

The point of this example is not to single out Ganeri but to illustrate just how dire the lack of representation of Sikh philosophy is. Even in philosophical engagement with the specific region in which Sikh philosophy originated, during the specific time period in which this philosophy originated, Sikh philosophy is completely ignored. In this way, the distinctive contributions of Sikh philosophy are erased from the narrative of history. Perhaps philosophers like Ganeri have simply overlooked the contributions of Sikh philosophy. Or perhaps they do not feel qualified to engage with it.

Either way, the erasure of Sikh philosophy is problematic. This Element is an attempt to address this problem, at least to some degree. My goal is to present a central component of Sikh philosophy, its ethics, by using the tools and methods of analytic philosophy to reconstruct it in a form that is understandable to Western audiences while still accurately capturing its distinctive, autochthonous features.

Of course, I do not expect readers to simply take my word that the Sikh tradition contains a distinctive philosophical system, including a systematic ethical theory. How can this claim be substantiated? In my view, it is to be substantiated through a rational reconstruction of the philosophical system contained in SGGS.[1] This idea can be applied to philosophical theories, in the following way: a rational reconstruction of a philosophical theory is an interpretation of it as a coherent system. If there is no coherent system to be found, the reconstruction fails. If the reconstruction succeeds, it offers proof that the theory presents a coherent system.

A rational reconstruction in this sense can be contrasted with a historical reconstruction. A historical reconstruction of a theory is an interpretation of that theory primarily in view of its historical and social context. As such, it presupposes no commitment to finding coherence or systematicity. Indeed, focusing on messy historical and social context may even push away from reconstructing a coherent and systematic theory, and toward deemphasizing the purely philosophical aspects of the development of the theory.

If there is doubt that Sikh philosophy presents a coherent and systematic ethical theory, this doubt must be addressed by engaging in interpretation of Sikh philosophy that attempts to draw out its coherence and systematicity. This is not something that has been attempted with Sikh philosophy, even by those

---

[1] The idea of rational reconstruction has its roots in the philosopher of science Imre Lakatos (1970), who originally applied it to theories in the history of science. See also Habermas (1979).

few philosophers who attempt to address it. For example, Arvind-Pal Singh Mandair, in his 2023 book on Sikh philosophy, engages in historical reconstruction rather than philosophical reconstruction. He is, in the first instance, engaged in a project of trying to understand the development of Sikh thought in historical and social context.

This leads Mandair to conclude that there is not a systematic philosophy contained in SGGS. Instead, it is "pre-philosophical," as he puts it (2023, 21). Moreover, he describes Sikh philosophy as an "assemblage," which developed from its "pre-philosophical roots" into a "field in its own right" through encounters with Western modernity (21). Whether or not Mandair's historiography is sound, he seems to have no background commitment to reconstructing a coherent philosophical system in his interpretive engagement with SGGS. Moreover, his characterization of the SGGS as pre-philosophical risks feeding into a Eurocentric conception of what is truly and systematically philosophical.[2] This example illustrates the pitfalls of historical reconstruction and the need for rational reconstruction when interpreting philosophical texts.

As a rational reconstruction, my approach begins with the assumption that there is a coherent and systematic ethical theory presented in SGGS. I then engage closely with the text with an eye toward drawing out this theory and presenting it so that its coherence and systematicity is clear to the reader. As brief background, SGGS consists of 1430 *ang* (pages) of verse, containing 5894 *sabad* (compositions). These compositions were primarily written by six of the ten Sikh gurus, who collectively founded the Sikh tradition over the course of roughly 200 years. The text also contains compositions from several Sikh devotees, as well as a number of religious progressives from Hindu and Muslim traditions. As such, it is in some ways unsurprising that many would be skeptical that such a text could contain a systematic and coherent philosophy.

Throughout my textual analysis, my claims about how the relevant theses, principles, and concepts fit together are guided by the methodology of analytic philosophy. That is, I attempt to provide clear and precise definitions of all terminology and provide rigorous arguments for my conclusions about how things must be interpreted in order to be coherent and systematic. Though the methodology I use is Western and Anglophone in its etiology, I attempt fastidiously to avoid superimposing any distinctively Western ideas, especially Judeo-Christian ones, onto Sikh ethics. As many Sikh scholars have noted, this has historically been a serious problem with attempts at interpreting Sikh thought.[3]

---

[2] This is ironic, given Mandair's explicit goal of providing a decolonized analysis. For a fuller version of this critique, see my review of Mandair's book (Singh 2024).

[3] See, e.g., N. G. K. Singh (2007).

So, while I attempt to clearly and precisely explicate the conceptual repertoire of Sikh ethics, I do not assume that these concepts have strict analogues in the conceptual repertoire of Western philosophy. Correspondingly, I advert to English translations of the relevant terms only when I am confident that doing so is reasonably innocuous. Finally, I reserve any comparative discussion of Sikh and Western philosophy (except in passing) for concluding remarks, so as to avoid giving the false impression that Sikh ethics must be legitimized through such comparisons.

On the matter of translation, the lack of accurate English translations of SGGS remains a notorious problem in Anglophone academic engagement with Sikh thought. As such, I provide my own translations of the original text throughout my analysis, sometimes drawing on existing translations, but always attempting to capture the original meaning as fully as possible.[4] One issue with many existing translations is that they attempt to render in English terms that have no accurate English translation. In such cases, I preserve the original terms and attempt to explain the concepts they pick out.

My exposition of Sikh ethics proceeds as follows. In Section 1, I provide a brief primer on the metaphysical foundations of Sikh philosophy, as I understand them. In Section 2, I explain some of the foundational concepts of Sikh ethics, such as *hukam*, *haumai*, and *sachiārā* and explain how they serve as distinctive building blocks for the Sikh ethical theory. In Section 3, I present my reconstruction of the Sikh theory of vice and virtue. As I understand it, there is a unity of both vices and virtues in Sikh ethics. Every vice has its source in *haumai*, the false conception of oneself as singularly important. Every virtue is an aspect of truthfulness – the virtue of the *sachiārā*. In Section 4, I present the Sikh theory of right conduct as truthful living and explain how virtue and rightness are systematically related. In Section 5, I explain how a variety of Sikh ethical practices are continuous with the ethical theory presented in SGGS.[5]

By drawing out a coherent and systematic ethical theory from SGGS, while remaining faithful to the text, I demonstrate that Sikh philosophy has such a theory to offer. While this conclusion will come as no surprise to many Sikh

---

[4]　I have relied heavily on SriGranth.org and SikhiToTheMax.org, two searchable online versions of SGGS, for the original Gurmukhi text, as well as its Roman transliteration, which was completed by Kulbir Singh Thind. The two existing translations I have drawn on are from Sant Singh Khalsa and Manmohan Singh, respectively. But both of these translations have significant problems, especially with importing Judeo-Christian conceptions. As such, my translations depart significantly from theirs in many places. For critical discussion of existing English translations, see N.G. K. Singh (2007), Jasjit Singh (2018), and Nirvikar Singh (2018).

[5]　Parts of this work, especially the theory of vice presented, draw upon work previously published in Singh (2021). I am grateful to Oxford University Press for providing permission to adapt that material here.

readers, it may come as a surprise to others, especially those not already familiar with Sikh thought. A further implication is the refutation of the view, prominent in the field of Sikh Studies, that Sikh ethical practices are discontinuous with what is espoused in SGGS. By showing how Sikh ethical practices function as extensions and applications of the Sikh ethical theory, I put serious pressure on the viability of this view.

My primary aim is not to directly defend Sikh ethics or convince readers of its truth. It is rather to prove that Sikh philosophy deserves a seat at the table when it comes to ethical theory, a seat which it has not yet been given in Anglophone analytic philosophy. For that to be the case, there must be a Sikh ethical theory that is coherent, systematic, and plausible. I hope the reader will be convinced that the theory of Sikh ethics presented in this Element has, at the very least, these three qualities.

1 Metaphysical Foundations

ੴ ਸਤਿ ਨਾਮੁ ਕਰਤਾ ਪੁਰਖੁ ਨਿਰਭਉ ਨਿਰਵੈਰੁ ਅਕਾਲ ਮੂਰਤਿ ਅਜੂਨੀ ਸੈਭੰ ਗੁਰ ਪ੍ਰਸਾਦਿ ॥
Ik oaṅkār sat nām kartā purakh nirbhao nirvair akāl mūrat ajūnī saibhaṅ gur parsād.

One Divine, whose name is Truth, source of all being, without fear, without enmity, existing beyond time, unborn, uncaused, [known] by the grace of the *guru*.

The above, known as *mūl mantar* (root verse), is the opening line of SGGS. In it, Guru Nanak presents the metaphysical foundations of the Sikh philosophy of Oneness. In order to understand Sikh ethics, it is necessary to understand at least the basics of this metaphysics, which I will attempt to present here. Though a deeper exploration of Sikh metaphysics is warranted, I will maintain the Element's focus on ethics and not undertake it here.

The cornerstone of Sikh metaphysics is the identification of the Divine, and of ultimate reality, with a single, all-encompassing Oneness. This is signified immediately by *ik oaṅkār* (ੴ). *Ik* means "one" and *oaṅkār* comes from *oaṅ* (cosmic sound or vibration) and *kār* (in this context meaning roughly "source," in the sense of the source of existence). Thus, *ik oaṅkār* represents a single fundamental entity at the bedrock of all existence. As Nikky-Guninder Kaur Singh puts it, *ik oaṅkār* "asserts existence ... and unity ... of the Ultimate Reality" (1981, 24). This fundamental Oneness is often referred to in SGGS simply as *ik* or *ek*: the One. The Divine is this ultimate reality.

Next, it is asserted that the name of the Divine is Truth– that is, the Divine is the truth (*sat*) itself – in particular, the fundamental truth of the Oneness of all existence. This will be of particular importance to understanding the place of truth in Sikh ethics. It will become clearer in the following sections why the identification of the Divine with this truth is foregrounded in the way it is. But the basic idea is that the idea of *truthful living* enjoined by Sikh ethics is to be understood as living the truth of Oneness.

The Divine, as fundamental Oneness, is then asserted to be the creator or source of all beings. This is sometimes understood as creation in a causal sense, as a creator God might create mankind (e.g., in Abrahamic conceptions of the Divine). However, such an understanding cannot capture the unity of existence asserted throughout SGGS. This is because causal relations are temporal and imply a separation between cause and effect. In light of this, while SGGS sometimes references a personified being engaging in the act of creation in this causal sense, such references are best understood as metaphorical. *Kartā purakh* must be understood not causally but constitutively. This is part of why I render *kartā* as *source* rather than creator. The true meaning of *kartā purakh* is to assert the metaphysical priority of the Divine over the myriad existing particulars in the world of ordinary experience. This constitutive relation between part and whole will also be crucial to my interpretation of Sikh ethics.

The phrases that follow *kartā purakh* in the *mūl mantar* are sometimes thought of as enumerating the qualities of the Divine. However, it is more informative to think of them as describing the qualities the Divine *lacks*. The Divine is devoid of fear and enmity, timeless, unborn and uncaused. Importantly, these are all qualities that define our existence as human beings. We are subject to causation, birth and death, our lives are temporal and temporary, and we experience emotions such as fear and enmity. These are the conditions of our existence at the level of individual, embodied subjects. But as the contrast with the Divine shows, they are not the conditions of our existence at the level of ultimate reality. As I will discuss later, this contrast between the conditions of our existence at these two levels is the source of both the problems of ethics and their solutions, according to Sikh ethics.

Though the core of Sikh metaphysics is presented in the very first line of SGGS, it is important to discuss a few crucial metaphysical concepts that are not contained in the *mūl mantar*. These are *dubidhā/dūjā* (duality), *māiā* (illusion), and *kūṛ* (falsehood). *Dubidhā* (lit., two modes) and *dūjā* (lit., other) both refer in context to the duality between self and other. The duality in question is a consequence of our embodied subjectivity. Because the boundaries of ordinary human experience are that of the individual subject, the subject experiences itself as a distinct entity, separate from the rest of existence, including other individuals. Addressing the Divine, the following passage suggests that duality is part of the condition of human existence, given the nature of the reality we ordinarily experience:

ਤੁਧੁ ਆਪੇ ਆਪੁ ਉਪਾਇਆ ॥
Tudh āpe āp upāiā.
You Yourself shaped this reality.

ਦੂਜਾ ਖੇਲੁ ਕਰਿ ਦਿਖਲਾਇਆ ॥
Dūjā khel kar dikhlāiā.
You constructed and staged the play of duality. (73)

Thus, *dubidhā/dūjā* refers to the duality between self and other that exists at the level of reality we ordinarily experience.

This duality is referred to throughout SGGS as being *māiā* – illusion:

ਦੂਜੀ ਮਾਇਆ ਜਗਤ ਚਿਤ ਵਾਸੁ ॥
Dūjī māiā jagat chit vās.
The *māiā* of duality inhabits the consciousness of [the people of] this world. (223)

This means that the duality between self and other is in some sense misleading, not deeply real. However, it does not assert that the world we experience and inhabit as individual subjects is wholly unreal, a complete illusion, as *māiā* is sometimes interpreted in Buddhist and Vedic thought. Rather, duality is an illusion in that, as W.H. McLeod puts it, "it is accepted for what it is not" (1968, 185). However, while McLeod interprets the illusion of *māiā* as one that obscures the impermanence of this world, I think this is not the right focus. The illusion of *māiā* is that of *dubidhā*, a fundamental separation between self and other. What is obscured by this illusion is that individual selves, though real, are not fundamental; in ultimate reality, there is no distinction between self and other. It is in seeing the world as fundamentally structured by the duality of self and other that we accept this duality for what it is not.

This brings us to *kūṛ*. *Kūṛ* (falsehood) is the opposite of *sat/sach* (truth or truthfulness). The term *kūṛ* is used extensively throughout SGGS, both in noun and adjectival form. In noun form, it tends to describe the false perception of a fundamental separation between self and other – the *māiā* of *dubidhā*. This falsehood is contrasted with the Divine truth of Oneness:

ਬਿਨੁ ਸਚੇ ਸਭ ਕੂੜੁ ਹੈ ਅੰਤੇ ਹੋਇ ਬਿਨਾਸੁ ॥੧॥ ਰਹਾਉ ॥
Bin sache sabh kūṛ hai ante hoe binās. ||1|| rahāo.
Without the True One, everything is falsehood; in the end, falsehood will be
   dispelled. ||1||Pause|| (49)

In adjectival form, *kūṛ* is applied both to instances of false duality and to the falseness of those attached to false duality:

ਵਿਣੁ ਸਚੇ ਸਭੁ ਕੂੜੁ ਕੂੜੁ ਕਮਾਈਐ ॥
viṇ sache sabh kūṛ kūṛ kamāīai.
Without the True One, all are false, and practice falsehood.

ਵਿਣੁ ਸਚੇ ਕੂੜਿਆਰੁ ਬੰਨਿ ਚਲਾਈਐ ॥

viṇ sache kūṛiār bann chalāīai.

Without the True One, the false are driven forth in bondage. (147)

All of this will be important in coming sections for understanding why *kūṛ* (falsehood) is used as a term of ethical criticism, in contrast to the virtue of truthfulness.

In light of the foregoing, Sikh metaphysics can be understood as a form of *priority monism* (the view that there is only one concrete object at the fundamental level), as opposed to *existence monism* (the view that there is only one concrete object, period).[6] At the level of ultimate reality, there is but one object: the Divine, the Truth, the One. However, this does not mean that the particular objects that seem to exist in the world as we experience it, including individuals, are unreal. Rather, it means that the existence of these particular objects is non-fundamental, posterior to the whole of *ik oa'nkār*.[7]

The above is crucial for properly understanding passages from SGGS such as the following:

ਸਭੁ ਕਿਛੁ ਆਪੇ ਆਪਿ ਹੈ ਦੂਜਾ ਅਵਰੁ ਨ ਕੋਇ ॥

Sabh kichh āpe āp hai dūjā avar na kōe.

The One itself is everything; there is no other at all. (39)

　　And:

ਦੂਜਾ ਕਉਣੁ ਕਹਾ ਨਹੀ ਕੋਈ ॥

Dūjā kauṇ kahā nahī koī.

Whom should I call the other? There is none.

ਸਭ ਮਹਿ ਏਕੁ ਨਿਰੰਜਨੁ ਸੋਈ ॥੧॥ ਰਹਾਉ ॥

Sabh mėh ek niranjan soī. ||1|| rahāo.

The Immaculate One is in all alike. ||1||Pause|| (223)

Out of context, such passages could easily be interpreted as wholesale denials of the existence of discrete individual selves. But within the full context of Sikh philosophy, this cannot be correct. As I discuss in the remaining sections, this would be incompatible with the ethical injunction to remain engaged (but in a particular way) with the world at the level of ordinary experience.

As I hope will become clear in the remainder of this Element, metaphysics and ethics are inextricably linked in Sikh philosophy. The metaphysical picture painted is one according to which the natural condition of human beings is

---

[6] This terminology comes from Schaffer (2010). The usefulness of Schaffer's distinction here was originally suggested to me by Sam Lebens.

[7] McLeod's (1968, 165) claim that the monistic interpretation of Sikh metaphysics must be rejected is, as I see it, a result of a failure to understand the distinction between these two forms of monism.

a kind of ignorance, in which our individual subjectivities prevent us from recognizing the truth of ultimate reality. Each individual falsely experiences the world as if their own significance is *sui generis*, even though in reality the significance of any individual can only be grounded in the whole. This falsehood gives rise to the central problem of ethics, the ultimate source of human wrongdoing, vice, and evil. The solution, and our duty, is to grasp and practice the truth of Oneness. How to accomplish this is the fundamental ethical question.

2 Ethical Foundations

ਸਚਹੁ ਓਰੈ ਸਭੁ ਕੋ ਉਪਰਿ ਸਚੁ ਆਚਾਰੁ ॥੫॥
Sachahu orai sabh ko upar sach āchār. ||5||
Truth is higher than everything; higher still is truthful living. ||5|| (62)

The ethical theory defended in Sikh philosophy is an ethic of truthful living. This line first asserts that truth (*sach*) is higher than everything. And yet, higher still is truthful living (*sach āchār*). What does this mean? In what sense can truth be higher than everything, if something else is higher still? The answer is that the fundamental truth of Oneness truly is the most important thing to grasp about the nature of reality. However, the sense in which truthful living is still higher is that a mere inner understanding of this fundamental truth is insufficient for living an ethical life. To live an ethical life, according to Sikh philosophy, requires not just knowing the truth of Oneness but *practicing* it. This is what is meant by truthful living.

Thus, the central ethical question is asked:

ਕਿਵ ਸਚਿਆਰਾ ਹੋਈਐ ਕਿਵ ਕੂੜੈ ਤੁਟੈ ਪਾਲਿ ॥
Kiv sachiārā hoīai kiv kūrhai tutai pāl.
How can one become a truthful person? How can the veil of falsehood be torn away?

ਹੁਕਮਿ ਰਜਾਈ ਚਲਣਾ ਨਾਨਕ ਲਿਖਿਆ ਨਾਲਿ ॥੧॥
Hukam rajāī chalnā Nānak likhiā nāl. ||1||
By walking in accordance with *hukam*, Nanak, so it is written. ||1|| (1)

In other words, the central question of Sikh ethics is how to live truthfully and become truthful, tearing away the veil of falsehood. The answer given in this passage is that one must walk in accordance with *hukam*.

2.1 Hukam

Hukam is a central concept in Sikh philosophy. I leave it untranslated, as there is no English term that fully captures the meaning of *hukam* as it is used in

SGGS. Following its Arabic/Persian roots and use in Islam, it is often translated as "command" or "will."[8] Mandair (2023) translates it instead as "imperative." However, all of these translations risk being significantly misleading.

If *hukam* is to mean "command" or "will," it must refer to a Divine command or will. Commands must be issued by someone, so for there to be a Divine command, the Divine must be the kind of entity that issues commands. But if the Divine is an all-encompassing Oneness that is unlike individual subjects in the various ways mentioned in the previous section, then the Divine is not the kind of entity that issues commands. Any sense in which the Divine issues commands would have to be metaphorical. Similar considerations hold for "will." For there to be a Divine will, the Divine must be the kind of entity that has a will. But again, the will, understood as an agential capacity, seems like the kind of thing we have in our embodiment as individuals, in contrast to the Divine. So, likewise, any sense in which the Divine has a will would have to be metaphorical.[9]

Similar problems arise for Mandair's conception of *hukam* as "imperative." While Mandair clarifies that *hukam* "refers less to the will of a deity endowed with personal consciousness than to a universal sense of being" (2023, 81), the need for this clarification illustrates how it is misleading to conceive of *hukam* as any kind of divine prescription. This is reinforced by a central and oft-quoted (including by Mandair) line from SGGS:

ਹੁਕਮੈ ਅੰਦਰਿ ਸਭੁ ਕੋ ਬਾਹਰਿ ਹੁਕਮ ਨ ਕੋਇ ॥
Hukmai anḍar sabẖ ko bāhar hukam na koe.
Everything exists within *hukam*, there is nothing outside of *hukam*. (1)

If everything exists within *hukam*, then it looks less like an imperative and more like a kind of natural order. According to Inderjit Kaur (2025), *hukam* encapsulates a natural order according to which all existence is interrelated, and nothing possesses ontological autonomy. This is more accurate, especially because Kaur uses the concept of a natural order to explain *hukam* rather than simply translating it as "order." On this interpretation, the order of *hukam* consists in the relation of all things to the ultimate reality of *ik oa'nkār*, and the consequent relation of those things to each other.[10]

---

[8] This is so in the translations of Bhai Manmohan Singh and Sant Singh Khalsa, both of which enjoy a status as the default English translations of SGGS (despite having serious shortcomings, in my view). Taran Singh (2001a) also translates *hukam* as "will."

[9] McLeod (1968, 201) makes similar points.

[10] McLeod (1968, 203) also understands *hukam* as a kind of order.

To "walk in accordance with *hukam*," then, is to live in a way that is true to this fundamental unity of reality. It is not, as might be thought from thinking of *hukam* as command, will, or imperative, to *obey* any kind of prescription. This is important to clarify, as the term can easily evoke Abrahamic conceptions of a personal God who issues commands. Despite its etymological roots in an Islamic context where such an understanding of *hukam* may be accurate, the conceptual role of *hukam* in Sikh ethics is distinct and does not imply a divine command ethical theory.

2.2 Haumai

This brings us to our next central ethical concept: *haumai*. Following the line quoted above, the next line of SGGS reads:

ਨਾਨਕ ਹੁਕਮੈ ਜੇ ਬੁਝੈ ਤ ਹਉਮੈ ਕਹੈ ਨ ਕੋਇ ॥੨॥
Nānak hukmai je bujhai ṯa haumai kahai na koe. ||2||
Nanak, one who understands *hukam* does not speak in *haumai*. (1)

This line sets up an opposition between *hukam*, the divine order of Oneness, and *haumai*. Like *hukam, haumai* lacks a neat English translation. It has been translated variously as ego, egotism, self-interest, and individuation. However, each of these terms only partially captures the concept. The most accurate attempt comes from Avtar Singh (1970, 23), who translates it as "I-am-ness." However, because this is not an ordinary English word, I elect to leave *haumai* untranslated and instead focus on elucidating its meaning.

Literally, *haumai* means something like "I am me." Essentially, it is a kind of false conception of oneself as singularly important, and correspondingly, a false conception of the world as revolving around oneself, as a world of objects there for one's use. At its extreme, it is a kind of ethical solipsism: an inability to conceive of anyone or anything but oneself as ultimately mattering. As we will see in the next section, *haumai* is the source of all vice and human evil in Sikh ethics.

This characterization shows how *haumai* relates to concepts like ego, egotism, self-interest, and individuation. In the sense referenced by translation of *haumai* as ego, it is a person's sense of self-esteem or self-importance. Egotism is, essentially, a sense of undue self-importance. Self-interest is what is to one's own advantage, without consideration of the good of others. And individuation refers to the demarcation of some discrete individual out of a larger whole. Though none of these terms fully captures the essence of *haumai*, each gets at aspects of it. In *haumai*, one foregrounds one's own ego and self-interest, losing consciousness of others as fellow ethical subjects. At the extreme, one individuates oneself so thoroughly from others that one comes to conceive of oneself as the only thing that ultimately matters.

As Avtar Singh notes, Sikh philosophy views *haumai* as part of the human condition:[11]

> The peculiarity of the human situation, according to Guru Nanak, lies in the fact that each person, in his empirical existence occupies himself with a narrow and limited viewpoint ... The problem for morality, or for that matter, for the whole of life, is how to widen or abscind this narrow or too-limited point of view ... (1970, 23)

Avtar Singh's use of the term "empirical existence" here is helpful. A person's empirical existence, I take it, is their existence at the level of reality they ordinarily observe and experience. This notion of empirical existence was referenced in the previous section, in the context of explaining *dubidhā/dūjā* (duality). There, I wrote that the experience of duality between self and other is a feature of individuated consciousness, which structures our ordinary experience.

It is out of this feature of our ordinary experience that *haumai*, the conception of oneself as having singular importance, arises:

ਸਦਾ ਸਦਾ ਤੂੰ ਏਕੁ ਹੈ ਤੁਧੁ ਦੂਜਾ ਖੇਲੁ ਰਚਾਇਆ ॥
Sadā sadā tūˈn ek hai tudh dūjā khel rachāiā.
For all eternity, you are One, but you created the play of duality.

ਹਉਮੈ ਗਰਬੁ ਉਪਾਇ ਕੈ ਲੋਭੁ ਅੰਤਰਿ ਜੰਤਾ ਪਾਇਆ ॥
Haumai garab upāe kai lobh antar jantā pāiā.
You created *haumai* and pride, and you placed greed within us. (139)

As this passage indicates, it is via the "play of duality" that *haumai* emerges out of Divine creation. This refers not to a personal God having imbued us with certain qualities but rather to the fact that *haumai* is a condition of our individual subjectivities emerging from the Oneness of the Divine.

Throughout SGGS, *haumai* is identified with a love of or attachment to duality:

ਦੁਰਜਨੁ ਦੂਜਾ ਭਾਉ ਹੈ ਵੇਛੋੜਾ ਹਉਮੈ ਰੋਗੁ ॥
Durjan dūjā bhāo hai vechhoṛā haumai rōg.
The evil person loves duality; they are separated through the disease of
  haumai. (1094)

In this and several other passages, *haumai* is described as *rōg* – a malady or disease. The disease of *haumai* is a psychological one: an inability to supersede the vision of reality presented in ordinary consciousness, according to which the boundaries of self also mark the limits of ethical significance. Mistaking the

---

[11] See also Taran Singh (2001b, 32–33).

duality of self and other for ultimate reality, the person who acts out of *haumai* is under the illusion that they are the sole subject in a world of objects. Because ultimate reality contains no such duality, only Oneness, the person who acts out of *haumai* acts out of ignorance of ultimate reality.

To sum up the picture painted so far: the central question of Sikh ethics is how to live truthfully. To live truthfully, it is said, one must follow *hukam*, the order of things. To follow *hukam*, one must transcend the natural condition of *haumai*. *Haumai* is the attachment to the self-other duality we experience in ordinary consciousness and is a natural condition of our existence as individuals with subjective experience. To mistake this self-other duality for ultimate reality is the fundamental ethical mistake.

2.3 Haumai within Hukam

The above account of *haumai* immediately raises two related questions. First, if *haumai* is the natural condition of our empirical existence, does that mean we must somehow transcend our empirical existence in order to transcend *haumai*? Second, if *haumai* is part of *hukam*, and *hukam* is the natural order of things within which everything falls, how can it be possible to transcend *haumai*? I will address these questions in turn.

The answer to the first question is, basically, *yes*. There is a sense in which we must transcend our empirical existence in order to transcend *haumai*. Because *haumai* is part of our natural condition, we cannot fully eradicate it while we remain embodied beings with individuated consciousness.[12] But we can substantially transcend *haumai* through connection with ultimate reality. By experiencing Oneness, however fleetingly, we can recognize the illusoriness of self-other duality and eschew *haumai*. But to experience Oneness, much is required, which I will explain in due course.

The details of the answer to the second question cannot be put off, if the relationship between *haumai* and *hukam* is to be intelligible. It will be helpful here to consider a slightly longer passage, which directly addresses such questions regarding the relationship between *haumai* and *hukam*:

ਹਉਮੈ ਏਹਾ ਜਾਤਿ ਹੈ ਹਉਮੈ ਕਰਮ ਕਮਾਹਿ ॥
Haumai ehā jāṯ hai haumai karam kamāhi.
It is the nature of *haumai* that people act out of *haumai*.

ਹਉਮੈ ਏਈ ਬੰਧਨਾ ਫਿਰਿ ਫਿਰਿ ਜੋਨੀ ਪਾਹਿ ॥
Haumai eī banḏẖnā fir fir jonī pāhi.
This is the bondage of *haumai*, a cycle of death and rebirth.

---

[12] My 2021 article on vice and virtue in Sikh ethics failed to make this point clear.

ਹਉਮੈ ਕਿਥਹੁ ਉਪਜੈ ਕਿਤੁ ਸੰਜਮਿ ਇਹ ਜਾਇ ॥
Haumai kithhu ūpjai kiṯ sanjam ih jāe.
From where does *haumai* originate? By what method can it be removed?

ਹਉਮੈ ਏਹੋ ਹੁਕਮੁ ਹੈ ਪਇਐ ਕਿਰਤਿ ਫਿਰਾਹਿ ॥
Haumai eho hukam hai paiai kiraṯ firāhi.
Haumai is that very *hukam*, in accordance with which it is our condition to wander.

ਹਉਮੈ ਦੀਰਘ ਰੋਗੁ ਹੈ ਦਾਰੂ ਭੀ ਇਸੁ ਮਾਹਿ ॥
Haumai ḏīragh rog hai ḏārū bhī is māhi.
Haumai is a chronic disease, but it also contains its own remedy.

ਕਿਰਪਾ ਕਰੇ ਜੇ ਆਪਣੀ ਤਾ ਗੁਰ ਕਾ ਸਬਦੁ ਕਮਾਹਿ ॥
Kirpā kare je āpṇī ṯā gur kā sabaḏ kamāhi.
With the grace of the Divine, one follows the *sabad* of the *gurū*.

ਨਾਨਕੁ ਕਹੈ ਸੁਣਹੁ ਜਨਹੁ ਇਤੁ ਸੰਜਮਿ ਦੁਖ ਜਾਹਿ ॥੨॥
Nānak kahai suṇhu janhu iṯ sanjam ḏukh jāhi. ||2||
Nanak says, listen, people: by this method, misery departs. ||2|| (466)

There are two interesting and important features of this passage that do have to be set aside, as they would take me too far afield to discuss. One is the reference to the cycle of death and rebirth, and the other is the concept of *sabad* (lit., word). Most important at this point is the assertion that *haumai* is part of *hukam*, and it is a disease that contains its own remedy.

The basic idea expressed in this passage is that, though *haumai* is part of the condition of our existence as individuals, these very same conditions include the prospect for transcending *haumai* by experiencing reality at a deeper level. In this way, the answer to the second question is posterior to the answer to the first. We can transcend *haumai* by making contact with ultimate reality. Thus, for it to be possible to transcend *haumai* even though it is part of *hukam*, it must be part of the nature of our relation to Oneness (and thus our relation to other individuals as parts of Oneness) that we can connect with it in some way. If the capacities we have as conscious subjects include such a capacity, then this is the sense in which *haumai*, even as it arises out of our nature as conscious subjects, contains its own cure. As I hope will become clear shortly, the very condition out of which *haumai* originates also gives us the tools to transcend it.

2.4 Haumai as Vice

Throughout SGGS, the notion of *haumai* is used to elucidate a theory of vice and virtue. In particular, it is claimed that cultivating virtue involves subduing *haumai* and gaining the ability to act, think, and feel in ways that transcend self-other duality. For example:

ਜਿਨਾ ਪੋਤੈ ਪੁੰਨੁ ਤਿਨ ਹਉਮੈ ਮਾਰੀ ॥
Jinā potai punn tin haumai mārī.
Those who have virtue as their treasure subdue haumai. (160)

The term used here for virtue is *punn*, which roughly means "goodness," in an aretaic sense (i.e., relating to the quality of one's character). The contrary term is *pāp*, which roughly means "evil," correspondingly in an aretaic sense. In Sikh philosophy, as in Western philosophy, these aretaic concepts pick out sustained traits of character that are cultivated through action:

ਪੁੰਨੀ ਪਾਪੀ ਆਖਣੁ ਨਾਹਿ ॥
Punnī pāpī ākhan nāhi.
Goodness and evil cannot be proclaimed.

ਕਰਿ ਕਰਿ ਕਰਣਾ ਲਿਖਿ ਲੈ ਜਾਹੁ ॥
Kar kar karnā likh lai jāhu.
It is through repeated action that they are inscribed. (4)

As such, unlike certain other central concepts of Sikh ethics (*haumai, hukam*), it is relatively innocuous to translate *punn* and *pāp* into English as goodness or virtue and evil or vice, respectively.

Virtue and vice, in these terms, are explicitly connected to duality:

ਪਾਪ ਪੁੰਨ ਕੀ ਸਾਰ ਨ ਜਾਣੀ ॥
Pāp punn kī sār na jāṇī
Those who do not understand the nature of vice and virtue

ਦੂਜੈ ਲਾਗੀ ਭਰਮਿ ਭੁਲਾਣੀ ॥
Dūjai lāgī bharam bhulāṇī.
wander astray, attached to duality. (110)

In this passage, attachment to duality is invoked as the fate of those who fail to understand virtue and vice. So, virtue has to do with overcoming attachment to duality.

There is another pair of contraries that roughly corresponds to the concepts of virtue and vice. In SGGS, the term *gun* (lit., quality) – in many contexts denotes good character traits. It is contrasted with *aogun* (lit., bad quality), which denotes bad character traits. These terms are also used to set up the opposition between *haumai* and virtue:

ਅਉਗਣੀ ਭਰਿਆ ਸਰੀਰੁ ਹੈ ਕਿਉ ਸੰਤਹੁ ਨਿਰਮਲੁ ਹੋਇ ॥
Augaṇī bhariā sarīr hai kio santahu nirmal hoe
The embodied individual is filled with vice; how, saints, can they become pure?

ਗੁਰਮੁਖਿ ਗੁਣ ਵੇਹਾਝੀਅਹਿ ਮਲੁ ਹਉਮੈ ਕਢੈ ਧੋਇ ॥

Gurmukh guṇ vehājhīah mal haumai kadhai dhoe.

The gurmukh, cultivating virtue, washes off the stain of *haumai*. (311)

This passage makes clear that *haumai* is the source of vice, and that transcending *haumai* is the key to becoming virtuous.

At this point, it is necessary to discuss another key distinction referenced in the above passage: the distinction between *gurmukh* and *manmukh*. Essentially, the *gurmukh* is the virtuous person and the *manmukh* is the vicious person. Literally, the *gurmukh* is someone who is *gurū*-facing, while the *manmukh* is someone who is self-facing. How does this distinguish between the virtuous person and the vicious person? The *gurmukh* is *gurū*-facing in the sense that their focus, in thought, action, and feeling, is on the *gurū*. In this context, *gurū* (lit. teacher, spiritual guide) refers not to any human *gurū* but to the ultimate *gurū*: the Divine, the One itself.

The *manmukh*, by contrast, is focused on their own *man* (lit., mind, will). In this context, *man* refers to the individuated and embodied consciousness. Thus, the *manmukh* is self-facing in the sense that they attach importance primarily or solely to themself *qua* individual. To use a more familiar English term, we might call the *manmukh* self-absorbed.[13] As a self-facing person, the *manmukh* is vicious precisely in the sense that they are consumed by *haumai*:

ਮਾਇਆ ਮੋਹਿ ਸਭੋ ਜਗੁ ਬਾਧਾ ॥

Māiā mohi sabẖo jag bāḏẖā.

Attached to *māiā*, the whole world is in bondage.

ਹਉਮੈ ਪਚੈ ਮਨਮੁਖ ਮੂਰਾਖਾ ॥

Haumai pacẖai manmukẖ mūrākẖā.

The foolish *manmukh* are consumed by *haumai*. (394)

This passage not only identifies the *manmukh* as consumed by *haumai* but also connects this condition to attachment to *māiā*. As discussed before, *māiā* is the illusion that self-other duality goes much deeper than it truly does. Thus, this passage further illuminates the relationship between *haumai* as vice, the *manmukh* as the vicious person, and the illusion of duality.

Moreover, the distinction between *gurmukh* and *manmukh* is explicitly identified with the virtue terms of *guṇ* and *aoguṇ*:

ਜਿਨ ਗੁਣ ਤਿਨ ਸਦ ਮਨਿ ਵਸੈ ਅਉਗੁਣਵੰਤਿਆ ਦੂਰਿ ॥

Jin guṇ tin sad man vasai aoguṇvantiā dūr.

[The *gurū*] dwells forever in the minds of the virtuous, far away from the vicious.

---

[13] *Manmukh* is also often translated as "self-willed," to capture the sense in which, acting selfishly, the *manmukh*'s will is turned inward. But the more literal translation is "self-facing."

ਮਨਮੁਖ ਗੁਣ ਤੈ ਬਾਹਰੇ ਬਿਨੁ ਨਾਵੈ ਮਰਦੇ ਝੂਰਿ ॥੨॥

Manmukh gun tai bāhre bin nāvai marde jhūr. ||2||

The *manmukh* are bereft of virtue. Without the Divine Name, they die in vain. ||2|| (27)

Recall that *haumai* is understood as a looking-inward to oneself as of primary or sole importance. While the virtuous understand the true nature of things, and thereby recognize the importance of others, the vicious cut themselves off from ultimate reality through their inability to transcend *haumai* and see outside of themselves. In the next Section, I will discuss how particular vices are rooted in *haumai*. But first, I must explain how virtue is illuminated by reference to the concept of *sachiārā*.

2.5 Truthfulness: The Virtue of the Sachiārā

Sachiārā denotes the truthful person. The adjectival form is *sachiār* – truthful. Among those writing on Sikh philosophy, the *sachiārā* is commonly recognized as one who has conquered *haumai*. Exploring this connection sheds further light on the systematicity of Sikh ethical concepts. The central question of Sikh ethics, presented in the opening stanzas of SGGS, is how to become *sachiārā*. This already suggests that truthfulness is the central virtue to which one should aspire in living an ethical life.[14] In SGGS, the terms used for truthfulness itself are the same terms used for truth – *sat* and *sach*. But it is the focus on becoming *sachiārā* that makes the centrality of truthfulness clear. This centrality is further substantiated by the connection with *haumai*. *Haumai* is the source of vicious action, thought, and feeling in Sikh ethics because it is based in falsehood. To act from *haumai* is to get things wrong; in this way, there is no gap in Sikh ethics between "wrong" understood as an ethical concept and "wrong" understood as false or incorrect.

This brings us back to the previous section's discussion of *kūṛ* (falsehood). As a reminder, *kūṛ* is used to describe both the perception of a fundamental self-other duality, and those who are attached to such a perception. Used in this way, *kūṛ* becomes a form of ethical criticism:

ਜਿਨਾ ਅੰਦਰਿ ਦੂਜਾ ਭਾਉ ਹੈ ਤਿਨ੍ਹਾ ਗੁਰਮੁਖਿ ਪ੍ਰੀਤਿ ਨ ਹੋਇ ॥

Jinā andar dūjā bhāo hai tinhā gurmukh parīt na hoe.

Those with love of duality in their hearts have no love for the *gurmukh*.

ਓਹੁ ਆਵੈ ਜਾਇ ਭਵਾਈਐ ਸੁਪਨੈ ਸੁਖੁ ਨ ਕੋਇ ॥

Ohu āvai jāe bhavāīai supnai sukh na koe.

They come and go, wandering without contentment even in their dreams.

---

[14] This is widely recognized by Sikh scholars. See Taran Singh (2001a) on the virtuous person as *sachiār* (truthful). Also, Kohli (1974, 35) writes that "truthfulness is the basic virtue." The centrality of truthfulness is also highlighted in Kaur (2025).

ਕੂੜੁ ਕਮਾਵੈ ਕੂੜੁ ਉਚਰੈ ਕੂੜਿ ਲਗਿਆ ਕੂੜੁ ਹੋਇ ॥
Kūṛ kamāvai kūṛ ucẖrai kūṛ lagiā kūṛ hoe.
They practice falsehood and utter falsehood; attached to falsehood, they become false.

ਮਾਇਆ ਮੋਹੁ ਸਭੁ ਦੁਖੁ ਹੈ ਦੁਖਿ ਬਿਨਸੈ ਦੁਖੁ ਰੋਇ ॥
Māiā moh sabẖ ḍukẖ hai ḍukẖ binsai ḍukẖ roe.
Attachment to *māiā* is total misery; in misery they perish and in misery they weep.

ਨਾਨਕ ਧਾਤੁ ਲਿਵੈ ਜੋੜੁ ਨ ਆਵਈ ਜੇ ਲੋਚੈ ਸਭੁ ਕੋਇ ॥
Nānak ḏẖāṯ livai joṛ na āvī je locẖai sabẖ koe.
Nanak, there can be no union between love of material things and love of the Divine, no
    matter how much everyone desires it.

ਜਿਨ ਕਉ ਪੋਤੈ ਪੁੰਨੁ ਪਇਆ ਤਿਨਾ ਗੁਰ ਸਬਦੀ ਸੁਖੁ ਹੋਇ ॥੨॥
Jin kao poṯai punn paiā ṯinā gur sabḏī sukẖ hoe. ||2||
Those who have the treasure of virtue find contentment in the *sabad* of the *gurū*. ||2|| (316)

This extended passage is illuminating because it connects *kūṛ* not just to the
metaphysical concepts of *ḏūjā* (duality) and *māiā* (illusion) but also to the
ethical concepts of *gurmukh* (the virtuous person) and *punn* (virtue/goodness).
In this passage, the vicious person is criticized as attached to falsehood and
practicing falsehood. Crucially, the falsehood they practice is the attachment to
false duality – that is, *haumai*. From the perspective of the person immersed in
haumai, the project of becoming *gurmukh* looks completely undesirable.

All of this is crucial to understanding why virtue is identified with truthfulness. Those who live falsely live in ignorance and rejection of the ultimate
reality of Oneness. On the contrary, those who live truthfully live in acceptance
of and connection with this ultimate reality. The *sachiārā* recognizes the
shallowness of self-other duality and seeks to eschew attachment to this duality.
They seek to live in a way that is true to the fundamental Oneness of all being.
Thus, the *sachiārā* and the *gurmukh* are one and the same. By contrast, the false
are trapped within their narrow, individualized point of view, deluded into
seeing "I am me" as ultimate reality. This is the sense in which *haumai* and
truthfulness are in opposition, and truthfulness is the fundamental virtue.

Because the *sachiārā* has conquered *haumai* and so achieved a form of higher
being, some scholars explicate the *sachiārā* as the *self-realized* person, rather
than the truthful person.[15] However, I think this is misleading for two reasons.
First, this less literal translation obscures the centrality of the concepts of truth
and truthfulness to Sikh ethics, and to Sikh philosophy in general. Second,
conceiving of the *sachiārā* as self-realized conflates self-realization and self-
transcendence. To be *sachiār* is to have transcended the narrow boundaries of

---

[15] See, e.g., Avtar Singh (1970, 23) and Mandair (2023, 82).

the individual self. Understanding the *sachiārā* as self-realized instead evokes a conception of higher being as a perfected individual self. However, to seek individual self-perfection would involve its own form of *haumai*.[16] As such, it is crucial to understand the *sachiārā* as truthful to the ultimate reality of Oneness, rather than as self-realized.

2.6 Conclusion

So far, I have attempted to draw out some of the distinctive foundations of the Sikh ethical system, focusing on three notions: *hukam* – the Divine order, *haumai* – the false sense of self-importance, and *sachiārā* – the truthful person. These concepts, along with the metaphysical foundations discussed in the previous section, are the starting points of Sikh ethics. Out of these concepts are built various further features of the Sikh ethical system: accounts of the particular vices and virtues, and of right and wrong action. These accounts are the focus of the next two sections.

3 Vice and Virtue

In this section, I will argue that there is both a unity of vices and a unity of virtues in Sikh ethics. All of the particular vices can be explained as manifestations of *haumai*, and all of the virtues can be explained as aspects of truthfulness. I discuss each of these unities in turn.

3.1 The Unity of the Vices

In discussion of the particular vices, Sikh ethics focuses on what are called in SGGS the "five thieves" (*panch chor*) – also sometimes the "five enemies" or "five evils." They are the vices of *kām* (lust), *krodh* (wrath), *lobh* (greed), *moh* (attachment), and *ahankār* (arrogance). Though I have presented translations for each of these vices for ease of explication, this is not because the English terms perfectly capture their exact nature. In this case, the English terms should be taken as close-enough counterparts, rather than precise equivalents. In fact, the exact meaning of these terms in Sikh ethics cannot be fully understood except by exploring what is said in SGGS about their connection to *haumai*.

That *haumai* is the source of these five vices is commonly assumed both in communal understanding, and in scholarly work on Sikhism. For example, Pashaura Singh writes:

> Traditionally, *haumai* is the source of five evil impulses: lust, anger, covetousness, attachment to worldly things, and pride. Under its influence humans

---

[16] I will return to this issue when I discuss the rejection of asceticism in Sikh ethics in Section 4.

become "self-willed" (*manmukh*), so attached to worldly pleasures that they forget the divine Name and waste their lives in evil and suffering. (2014, 231)

Indeed, it seems fairly uncontroversial in both the community and the literature that *haumai* is the source of these five primary vices in Sikhism.[17] However, perhaps precisely because it is so uncontroversial, textual evidence for this claim is rarely provided. Unfortunately, this leaves it obscure to those who are not already familiar with the Sikh tradition. Thus, as with all of the central theses of Sikh ethics, I present key passages from SGGS as textual support. These passages illuminate how each vice has its source in *haumai*.

Several passages in SGGS make explicit the connection between *haumai* and these five vices. For example:

ਇਸੁ ਦੇਹੀ ਅੰਦਰਿ ਪੰਚ ਚੋਰ ਵਸਹਿ ਕਾਮੁ ਕ੍ਰੋਧੁ ਲੋਭੁ ਮੋਹੁ ਅਹੰਕਾਰਾ ॥

Is dehī andar panch chor vaseh kām krodh lobh moh ahankārā.

Within this body dwell the five thieves: lust, wrath, greed, attachment, and arrogance.

ਅੰਮ੍ਰਿਤੁ ਲੂਟਹਿ ਮਨਮੁਖ ਨਹੀ ਬੂਝਹਿ ਕੋਇ ਨ ਸੁਣੈ ਪੁਕਾਰਾ ॥

Amrit lūteh manmukh nahī būjheh koe na suṇai pūkārā.

They plunder the sacred nectar, but the *manmukh* does not realize; no one hears their cries.

ਅੰਧਾ ਜਗਤੁ ਅੰਧੁ ਵਰਤਾਰਾ ਬਾਝੁ ਗੁਰੂ ਗੁਬਾਰਾ ॥੨॥

Andhā jagat andh vartārā bājh gurū gubārā. ||2||

The world is ignorant, its customs are ignorant; without the *Guru*, it is in darkness. ||2||

ਹਉਮੈ ਮੇਰਾ ਕਰਿ ਕਰਿ ਵਿਗੁਤੇ ਕਿਹੁ ਚਲੈ ਨ ਚਲਦਿਆ ਨਾਲਿ ॥

Haumai merā kar kar vigute kihu chalai na chaldiā nāl.

Acting out of *haumai* and possessiveness they are ruined; when they depart, nothing goes with them. (600)

And:

ਜਿਨੑੀ ਨਾਮੁ ਵਿਸਾਰਿਆ ਕੂੜੇ ਕਹਣ ਕਹੰਨੑਿ ॥

Jinhī nām visāriā kūṛe kahan kaha'nnih.

Those who forget the Divine Name are said to be false.

ਪੰਚ ਚੋਰ ਤਿਨਾ ਘਰੁ ਮੁਹੰਨੑਿ ਹਉਮੈ ਅੰਦਰਿ ਸੰਨੑਿ ॥

Panch chor tinā ghar muhnih haumai andar sannih.

The five thieves plunder their homes as *haumai* breaks in.

ਸਾਕਤ ਮੁਠੇ ਦੁਰਮਤੀ ਹਰਿ ਰਸੁ ਨ ਕਹੰਨੑਿ ॥

Sākat muthe durmatī har ras na jāṇannih.

The materialistic people are deceived by ill-will; they do not know the essence of the Divine. (854)

---

[17] See the entry on the five evils in *The Encyclopedia of Sikhism* (ed. Harbans Singh 2011, vol. 2, 29–34).

Though these passages do not go so far as to overtly assert that *haumai* is the source of the five vices, they illustrate it in the poetic fashion characteristic of SGGS. For example, the "home" that is plundered is a poetic reference to the self. And it *is* made explicit in these passages that *haumai* is not to be understood as just another particular vice.

The first passage asserts plainly that those who manifest particular vices are "acting out of *haumai*." The second passage more metaphorically expresses the same thing. Thus, it is fair to infer from these passages, as well as the ample scriptural evidence linking *haumai* to vice in general, that *haumai* is to be understood as the source of the five vices. It is less straightforward to glean *how* in particular each vice is thought to manifest *haumai*. Nevertheless, such an explanation can be reconstructed through further textual examination, taking each of the five vices in turn.

3.1.1 Kām

I have translated *kām* as lust. It is also sometimes translated as "sexual desire," or "concupiscence," but these are poor translations. The former is straightforwardly inaccurate, as not all sexual desire is considered vicious by Sikhism, and the latter is too closely tied to Catholic theology.[18] Lust, though not perfect, is much more accurate to the meaning of *kām*, because of how it is contrasts with love. Sikhism does not in any way reject healthy, loving sexual desire; in fact, as I will discuss later, Sikhism eschews asceticism and self-denial. When *kām* is criticized, it is clear from context that it denotes a kind of sexual obsession or objectifying sexual desire:

ਅਹਿਨਿਸਿ ਕਾਮਿ ਵਿਆਪਿਆ ਵਣਜਾਰਿਆ ਮਿਤ੍ਰਾ ਅੰਧੁਲੇ ਨਾਮੁ ਨ ਚਿਤਿ ॥
Ahinis kām viāpiā vaṇjāriā miṯrā andhule nām na chit.
You are continuously engrossed in lust, merchant friend, and your
    thoughts ignore the Divine Name. (75)

And:

ਕਾਮਵੰਤ ਕਾਮੀ ਬਹੁ ਨਾਰੀ ਪਰ ਗ੍ਰਿਹ ਜੋਹ ਨ ਚੁਕੈ ॥
Kāmvant kāmī baho nārī par garih joh na chūkai.
The lustful, lecherous person desires many others and cannot stop peeking
    into their homes. (672)

These passages are typical of how *kām* is discussed in SGGS. What they describe is not just any sort of sexual desire but an obsessive, objectifying lust.

---

[18] In general, translations of SGGS have tended to use Christian terms in various places, perhaps to make the text more intelligible to Western audiences. I reject this approach and have tried as much as possible to avoid it.

The first passage describes *kām* as something the addressee is "continuously engrossed in," to the point that they are not able to keep the Divine Name in view. The mention of the Divine Name here is important, because it refers to the name of the ultimate truth (*sat nām*) of Oneness (*ik oa'nkār*). Therefore, what is said here is that *kām* is the kind of desire that is incompatible with a recognition of Oneness. This is because *kām* is the kind of desire that is held toward something as an object – a thing that exists to gratify the subject. This is the sense in which *kām* is specifically *objectifying* sexual desire.

The second passage reinforces this message with a concrete example: the lecher who peeks into women's homes clearly desires them merely as objects of his sexual gratification. Such objectifying sexual desire, which I mean to pick out by translating *kām* as "lust," manifests an attachment to self-other duality. The lustful person conceives of himself as the sole subject, and the object of his desire as a mere object. This explains how the lustful person is *manmukh*. He is self-facing in the sense that he attaches importance to himself *qua* individual, but in viewing the other as a mere object attaches no real importance to the other.

Once we attend to the objectifying nature of *kām*, it becomes clear how it manifests *haumai*. *Haumai*, at its extreme, is essentially a false conception of oneself as the only real subject in a world of objects there for one's use. It is in its objectification that lust manifests *haumai*.[19] Connecting *kām* to objectifying sexual desire in particular not only illuminates its nature and relationship to *haumai* but also provides a blueprint for understanding how the other vices manifest *haumai*. Using this blueprint to analyze the other vices illuminates a unified explanation of the vices in terms of *haumai*. Not only do all the vices manifest *haumai* but *how* they manifest it is, at a general level, the same.

3.1.2 Krodh

I have translated *krodh* as "wrath." It sometimes gets translated as "unresolved anger," or simply "anger," though neither of these is quite right. In SGGS, *kām* and *krodh* are often discussed together:

ਹਉ ਰੋਗੁ ਬਿਆਪੈ ਚੁਕੈ ਨ ਭੰਗਾ ॥
Hao rog biāpai chukai na bhangā.
The disease of *haumai* clings to them, and their faults are not removed.

ਕਾਮ ਕ੍ਰੋਧ ਅਤਿ ਤ੍ਰਿਸਨ ਜਰੰਗਾ ॥
Kām krodh ati trisan jarangā.
They burn with lust, wrath, and appetitive desire. (1305)

---

[19] Western philosophers have more recently pointed out how sexual objectification can be wrong in congenial ways. See, e.g., Nussbaum (1995).

This passage is from a composition describing people who go on fasts, take pilgrimages, and practice ritualistic postures. We might wonder why these people would be filled with wrath. This will become clear in the next section, when I discuss Sikh ethics' rejection of asceticism. For now, it is further evidence that the vices at issue here are more specific than simply "anger" or "sexual desire."

In the above passage, *kām* and *krodh* are connected not just to *haumai* but also to *trisnā* (lit. thirst, yearning), which refers to appetitive desire. Thus, the focus here is on *kām* and *krodh* as appetitive desires. That *kām* is an appetitive desire has already been made clear in the previous discussion. But examining how *krodh* refers specifically to an appetitive desire is helpful for illuminating its nature, and why it is seen as similarly related to *haumai*.

Like sexual desire, not all anger is considered vicious in the Sikh tradition. For example, there is nothing necessarily wrong with righteous anger at injustice.[20,21] As loving sexual desire is to be distinguished from objectifying lust, so righteous anger at injustice is to be distinguished from appetitive wrath. Consider what it means for wrath to be an appetite: it must consist in a desire for some kind of gratification (like sexual gratification in the case of lust). The wrathful person is gratified when the object of their desire suffers. Wrath is an appetite for the suffering, usually through some kind of retribution or punishment, of its object. It is because descriptions of *krodh* in SGGS fit with this conception of wrath that I take it to be the most appropriate translation.

Throughout SGGS, *krodh* is contrasted with both compassion and forgiveness. For example:

ਹੇ ਕਲਿ ਮੂਲ ਕ੍ਰੋਧੰ ਕਦੰਚ ਕਰੁਣਾ ਨ ਉਪਰਜਤੇ ॥
He kal mūl krodh'n kadanch karuṇā na uparjate.
Wrath, you are the root of strife; compassion never wells up in you.

ਬਿਖਯੰਤ ਜੀਵੰ ਵਸੰ ਕਰੋਤਿ ਨਿਰਤ੍ਯੰ ਕਰੋਤਿ ਜਥਾ ਮਰਕਟਹ ॥
Bikhyant jīv'n vasyy'n karot nirtyy'n karot jathā maraktėh.
You control sinful creatures and make them dance like monkeys. (1358)

And:

ਗੁਰਿ ਮਿਲਿਐ ਹਮ ਕਉ ਸਰੀਰ ਸੁਧਿ ਭਈ ॥
Gur miliai ham kao sarīr sudh bhaī.
Meeting the *gurū*, I came to have awareness of myself.

---

[20] For agreement, see the entry on *krodh* in *The Encyclopedia of Sikhism* (ed. Harbans Singh 2011, vol. 2, 531–532). One might also interpret Guru Gobind Singh's *Zafarnāmā* as expressing righteous indignation at injustice.

[21] Related points have been made by contemporary Western philosophers – for example, Frye (1983) and Cherry (2021).

ਹਉਮੈ ਤ੍ਰਿਸਨਾ ਸਭ ਅਗਨਿ ਬੁਝਈ ॥

Haumai ṭrisnā sabḥ agan bujḥī.

All of the fires of *haumai* and appetitive desire have been quenched.

ਬਿਨਸੇ ਕ੍ਰੋਧ ਖਿਮਾ ਗਹਿ ਲਈ ॥੭॥

Binse kroḍh kḥimā gèh laī. ‖7‖

Wrath has perished, and I have grasped hold of forgiveness. ‖7‖ (233)

These descriptions paint a picture of *krodh* as the kind of wrath referenced above, in which one would be gratified by the suffering of the offender in the form of retribution or punishment. Moreover, this gratification seems to reflect the false perception that one has been somehow made lower than the offender, and the offender needs to suffer to correct this. This understanding of wrath helps make clear how it manifests *haumai*: the wrathful person wants to hurt others to improve his own status or make himself feel better.[22] Insofar as he is concerned with his own status as compared to others, he is attached to self-other duality.

This understanding of *krodh* also illuminates why righteous anger at injustice is not necessarily vicious. From a Sikh perspective, anger can only be righteous if it is not born of *haumai*. This means righteous anger cannot consist in the desire to improve one's own status, or for the offender to suffer in order to be brought down in relative status. Nor can it consist in any kind of appetite that aims at its own gratification. Righteous anger can only consist in a strong motivation to correct injustice and must be born out of the subject's care for all beings as One. There is nothing false about being motivated by the perception of injustice, and such motivation may even be necessary for fighting injustice. As I will return to later, this is a form of engagement with the world that is seen as obligatory in Sikh ethics. So, not all anger can be vicious. Importantly, however, *krodh* is seen as the default, vicious form of anger, while virtuous anger is a kind of reformed emotion of the *sachiārā*.

3.1.3 Lobh

Lobh, which I have translated as greed, is relatively straightforward as a manifestation of *haumai*. It is understood not just as the desire to have more possessions but also the desire to take things from others. The avaricious person sees the world around him as a world of objects for his use; he fails to take into account the needs of others. At its extreme, his greed makes him see other people too as mere objects – he becomes an ethical solipsist:

---

[22] Nussbaum (2016) attributes a similar conception of anger in general to Aristotle and criticizes anger as pernicious. Though there are similarities here, Sikh ethics criticizes what I have been calling wrath in particular, as opposed to righteous anger.

ਕਰਮੁ ਨ ਜਾਣਾ ਧਰਮੁ ਨ ਜਾਣਾ ਲੋਭੀ ਮਾਇਆਧਾਰੀ ॥
Karam na jāṇā dharam na jāṇā lobhī māiādhārī.
I know neither *karam* nor *dharam*; out of greed, I chase illusory possessions. (624)

One instructive feature of this line is that it connects greed to ignorance of *karam* (good deeds) and *dharam* (right conduct), making explicit the connection between the aretaic (vice, virtue), the evaluative (good, bad), and the deontic (right, wrong). The avaricious person, consumed by the desire for material possessions, is ignorant of what he ought to do. Moreover, what he chases is illusory (*maiā*), because his desire is predicated on self-other duality. Acting in *haumai*, the *manmukh* can only look inward to his own appetites and selfish desires.

3.1.4 Moh

Unlike *lobh*, *moh* is somewhat less straightforward. I have translated it as "attachment," which is the standard translation. However, this is imperfect given the broad meaning of "attachment" in the English language. Immediately evoked is the idea that all worldly entanglements are vicious, and that the virtuous person must eschew them. While this plays into a conception of Eastern philosophical traditions that is common in the West, it is particularly important to avoid in the case of Sikhism, which explicitly denies this conception of virtue. Sometimes *moh* is instead translated as "emotional attachment" in particular, which does a somewhat better job of picking out the phenomenon in question. But this still risks suggesting the inaccurate view that one should eschew all worldly entanglements, such as love for family and friends.

Sikh ethics does not prescribe ascetic self-denial, or enjoin us not to live in the world. Caring about worldly things, especially other people, cannot be the kind of emotional attachment that *moh* refers to. To understand what kind of attachment *moh* refers to, we must understand its object. The most common object of *moh* mentioned in SGGS is *maiā* itself – the illusion of self-other duality:

ਮਾਇਆ ਮੋਹੁ ਗੁਬਾਰੁ ਹੈ ਤਿਸ ਦਾ ਨ ਦਿਸੈ ਉਰਵਾਰੁ ਨ ਪਾਰੁ ॥
Māiā moh gubār hai tis dā na disai urvār na pār.
Attachment to *maiā* is an ocean of darkness; neither this shore nor the other can be seen.

ਮਨਮੁਖ ਅਗਿਆਨੀ ਮਹਾ ਦੁਖੁ ਪਾਇਦੇ ਡੁਬੇ ਹਰਿ ਨਾਮੁ ਵਿਸਾਰਿ ॥
Manmukh agiānī mahā dukh pāide dube har nām visār.
The ignorant *manmukh* suffer great pain; forgetting the Divine Name, they drown. (89)

The message of passages such as this one is that emotional attachment to *maiā* keeps one in ignorance of the ultimate reality of Oneness. As a reminder, the concept of *maiā* in Sikh philosophy tends to refer specifically to the illusion that the world as we experience it, with all of its self-other duality, is all there is to reality.

The above helps to make sense of various other passages in SGGS where the apparent object of *moh* is not *maiā* itself but things like household and family. Taken in isolation, such passages may seem to be in conflict with Sikh ethics' rejection of asceticism. However, if we understand the problematic kind of attachment to things like household and family as attachment under the aspect of *maiā*, the apparent conflict vanishes. What is vicious is not caring about one's family but rather being emotionally attached to them as *things*, as objects. The *manmukh* sees their significance as being apart from his, and thus they can be treated as extensions of his individual will and desire. Thus, he substitutes the priority of himself over others for the priority of the Divine over all individuated selves. This shows how *moh*, in creating a false duality between oneself as subject and the world as one of mere objects, manifests *haumai*.

3.1.5 Ahankār

Finally, we come to *ahankār*, which I have translated as "arrogance." It is sometimes translated as "ego" or "egotism" as well, but this is too general and risks simply identifying *ahankār* with *haumai*. Nevertheless, *ahankār* has a particularly close relation to *haumai*. It does not require much explanation to see how inflated self-regard and a tendency to view things in terms of one's own status and recognition manifest a false conception of one's own importance. So, it will not be necessary to say much in defense of the claim that arrogance manifests *haumai*.

Indeed, *ahankār* is so closely related to *haumai* that it can sometimes help illuminate how other vices, like *krodh* and *lobh*, have their source in *haumai*. One might point out that *krodh* and *lobh* manifest *haumai* because they involve a desire for status and recognition, a desire to be above others. However, this is less clear when it comes to *kām* and *moh*, neither of which necessarily has to do with status and recognition. In some cases, both *kām* and *moh* seem to be motivated by something more like insecurity or lack of healthy self-esteem, rather than by arrogance. Perhaps this is even true of some cases of *krodh* and *lobh* as well. This helps to show why *ahankār* is not the same as *haumai*. While vices can be always explained in terms of *haumai*, they cannot always be explained in terms of *ahankār*, even if they are sometimes closely related to it. Though arrogance is perhaps the paradigm case of misunderstanding one's own significance in relation to others, it is not the only one.

3.2 The Unity of the Virtues

I now turn to the unity of the virtues in Sikh ethics. This is a somewhat more complex issue than that of the unity of the vices. In the case of the vices, there is near universal agreement among scholars and practitioners that they have their source in *haumai*. Thus, establishing the unity of the vices has been a matter of providing textual evidence and further explanation for an uncontroversial thesis. Moreover, SGGS itself delimits the task by providing, in the form of the five thieves, a set of particular vices that *haumai* is supposed to explain.

There is no corresponding list of virtues presented so neatly in SGGS, which makes understanding the unity of the virtues more of an interpretive undertaking. As a result, there has not been as much scholarly consensus about the virtues as there has been about the vices. As I argue, the particular virtues are unified by their relationship to truthfulness – the virtue of the *sachiārā*. In this way, truthfulness is contrary to *haumai*, which unifies vice. While *haumai* reflects attachment to self-other duality and disconnection from ultimate reality, to be truthful is to transcend self-other duality and connect with ultimate reality. Though I am not the first to hold that truthfulness is the fundamental virtue in Sikh ethics, my novel contribution is a comprehensive explanation of how truthfulness unifies the particular virtues.

One obstacle to such an explanation is the prominence of the mistranslation of *sachiārā* as the self-realized person rather than the truthful person. This can be set aside, as it has already been discussed. However, there is another obstacle, which is that truthfulness itself is sometimes identified with the much narrower, particular virtue of honesty or veracity. For example, in Avtar Singh's discussion of the virtues, he identifies truthfulness as but one of several particular virtues. In doing so, he argues that the virtue of truthfulness "ought to be distinguished from 'Truth' in the metaphysical sense" (1970, 89). The upshot of this claim is that truthfulness as a virtue has nothing to do with the fundamental truth of Oneness in Sikh philosophy.

This interpretation cannot be correct. While Avtar Singh is surely correct that honesty or veracity can be understood as a particular virtue, this cannot be what is meant when discussing the virtuous person as *sachiārā*. To understand truthfulness in that way would foreclose the integration of metaphysics and ethics that is crucial to Sikh philosophy. Contrary to such an interpretation, truthfulness must be understood in the broad metaphysical sense of living in a way that is true to Oneness.

The problem with Avtar Singh's interpretation can be seen in how it handles the important line quoted in the previous section:

ਸਚਹੁ ਓਰੈ ਸਭੁ ਕੋ ਉਪਰਿ ਸਚੁ ਆਚਾਰੁ ॥੫॥

Sachahu orai sabh ko upar sach āchār. ||5||

Truth is higher than everything; higher still is truthful living. ||5|| (62)

Though he also quotes this line, he treats it as if it espouses truthful living (*sach āchār*) merely in relation to a particular virtue. This is difficult to make sense of, given that the whole point of this line is to say that truthful living is the highest ideal. This would be incoherent if truthfulness were just another virtue on the same level as all the particular virtues.[23] We can only make sense of the fundamentality of the question "how does one become truthful?" and the assertion of truthful living as the highest ideal, if we interpret truthfulness as the fundamental virtue. Moreover, as I show in the following sections, truthfulness understood in this way unifies the particular virtues that receive most attention in SGGS.

Again, there is no neat list of virtues in SGGS to parallel the five thieves. This leaves scholars of Sikh ethics to glean a list from the many verses that discuss particular virtues. Avtar Singh, for example, lands on "wisdom, truthfulness, temperance, courage, justice, humility and contentment" as the particular virtues to be discussed, though he does not claim this list is exhaustive (1970, 81). Following him, Gurnam Kaur Bal (2017) employs an identical taxonomy of virtues in Sikh ethics.[24]

The list of particular virtues I discuss is similar, but not exactly the same. First, as I have explained, I take truthfulness to be the fundamental virtue in Sikh ethics, rather than one of the particular virtues. Second, I set aside courage (*sūrā*) and justice (*niāo*). Though both can be seen as virtues in Sikh ethics, my goal is for this discussion to reflect the focus of the primary text. Courage and justice are discussed in SGGS, but not generally in the context of ascribing virtues. Courage is mostly invoked in the course of using the metaphor of the brave warrior to describe those who conquer *haumai*. Justice is largely discussed as a property of states of affairs, rather than as a character trait. However, I will return to justice in Section 5, when discussing Sikh ethical practices. Finally, again attempting to follow the focus of SGGS, I will discuss the virtue

---

[23] Unfortunately, this misinterpretation has been accepted by others writing about virtue in Sikh ethics. For example, Gurnam Kaur Bal's encyclopedia article on virtue follows Avtar Singh's taxonomy of the virtues, quoting and endorsing his interpretation of the role of truthfulness. She claims that *sach/sat* is used in different senses as an attribute of the divine and as a moral virtue, as if these senses are disunified (2017, 462).

[24] For yet another taxonomy of virtues, see Kohli (1974). As mentioned in Section 2, his analysis agrees with mine in that he argues that "truthfulness is the basic virtue" (35). However, Kohli attempts to find five "cardinal virtues" that correspond to the five thieves, and in doing so, does not focus on which virtues are explicitly emphasized in SGGS. Kohli also argues that the path to virtue is one of "self-realisation or Perfectionism," which I have argued cannot be correct.

of *daiā* (compassion), as well as focusing specifically on *bibek* (discernment) rather than the more general *giān* (wisdom).

This leaves me with five particular virtues to discuss: *daiā* (compassion), *santokh* (contentment), *sanjam* (self-control), *saram* (humility), and *bibek* (discernment). As with the particular vices, these English terms should be taken as close-enough counterparts, rather than perfect equivalents. As the nature of the particular vices was illuminated by drawing out their connection to *haumai*, so too the nature of these particular virtues is illuminated by drawing out their connection to truthfulness. I contend that all of these virtues can be understood as aspects of truthfulness to the ultimate reality of Oneness.[25]

3.2.1 Daiā

Daiā is standardly translated as compassion, kindness, or benevolence.[26] This virtue is also sometimes referred to in SGGS using the term *karuṇā*, including in a passage quoted in the earlier discussion of *krodh*, which sets wrath up in opposition to compassion. *Daiā* is mentioned early in SGGS, where it is made clear that it is an important virtue:

ਧੌਲੁ ਧਰਮੁ ਦਇਆ ਕਾ ਪੂਤੁ ॥
Dhoul dharam ḍaiā kā pūt.
The mythical bull is *dharam*, the son of compassion;

ਸੰਤੋਖੁ ਥਾਪਿ ਰਖਿਆ ਜਿਨਿ ਸੂਤਿ ॥
Santokh thāp rakhiā jin sūt.
it patiently keeps the order of the world.

ਜੇ ਕੋ ਬੁਝੈ ਹੋਵੈ ਸਚਿਆਰੁ ॥
Je ko bujhai hovai sachiār.
They who understand this become truthful. (3)

This passage asserts that *dharam* (right conduct) is the son of compassion. I take the filial relation here to be a metaphor for motivation: what is being said here is that right conduct is motivated by compassion. Compassion, through motivating right conduct, keeps the order of the world (i.e., *hukam*).[27] Linking *daiā* to *dharam* in this way makes its importance clear. The passage then explicitly

---

[25] Of course, this is not exactly the same as establishing that all virtues can be understood in this way, because there could be other virtues. But the fact that the virtues that are foregrounded in SGGS can all be understood in this way provides strong evidence for the more general claim.

[26] *Daiā* is also sometimes translated as "mercy," but this has misleading connotations in English, especially given that it is likely to evoke Christian or at least broadly Abrahamic associations.

[27] The metaphor of the "mythical bull" is perhaps a reference to *Kuyūta*, the cosmic bull in medieval Islamic philosophy that helps to hold up the Earth. In the above passage, just as the mythical bull is said to physically hold the Earth in place, *dharam* holds it in place ethically.

connects *daiā* to being *sachiār*: those who understand the importance of compassion become truthful.

Compassion is explicitly connected to truthfulness elsewhere as well:

ਸਚੁ ਤਾ ਪਰੁ ਜਾਣੀਐ ਜਾ ਸਿਖ ਸਚੀ ਲੇਇ ॥
Sach tā par jāṇīai jā sikẖ sachī lei.
Truth is understood only by those who accept the true teachings.

ਦਇਆ ਜਾਣੈ ਜੀਅ ਕੀ ਕਿਛੁ ਪੁੰਨੁ ਦਾਨੁ ਕਰੇਇ ॥
Daiā jāṇai jīa kī kichh punn dān karei.
Knowing compassion, they virtuously engage in beneficent deeds. (468)

This passage links compassion not only to truth (*sach*) but also to virtue in general (*punn*). It is not difficult to see how being compassionate is a component of being true to ultimate reality in Sikh ethics. To be compassionate is to care for others as one cares for oneself. If all dualities of self and other are illusory at the level of ultimate reality, then compassion is a way of recognizing this ultimate truth and living it in one's actions. Whereas the *manmukh*, engrossed in *haumai*, selfishly directs his care and concern inwards, the *gurmukh* has care and concern for everyone, as all are ultimately One. Thus, *daiā* in Sikh ethics is compassion in the sense of universal care and concern for others. It is not only explicitly contrasted with the particular vice of *krodh* as in the earlier passage but also in other places with *kām* and *ahankār*.[28]

3.2.2 Santokh

Santokh is standardly translated as contentment, though it can also mean satisfaction or even patience. It often appears alongside *daiā* in discussions of virtue in SGGS. For example:

ਸਤੁ ਸੰਤੋਖੁ ਦਇਆ ਕਮਾਵੈ ਏਹ ਕਰਣੀ ਸਾਰ ॥
Sat santokh daiā kamāvai eh karṇī sār.
The practices of true contentment and compassion, these are the worthy actions. (51)

Here, the connection between the virtues of contentment and compassion, and the worth of actions is made clear, as is the connection with truth (*sat*). Moreover, the fact that these two virtues are often discussed together is instructive. There is a relation between the compassionate person and the contented person. The contented person is contented because they lack excessive appetites, which in Sikh ethics are always fueled by excessive self-regard (i.e.,

---

[28] See, e.g., SGGS 51 and 379. Those passages also contrast these vices with *santokh* (contentment) and connect both *daiā* and *santokh* to *sat* (truth).

haumai). As a result, the contented person has plenty of room in their consciousness for care and concern for others.

By contrast, if one has excessive appetitive desire, this crowds out one's ability to care for others as one cares for oneself. This is why the person without *santokh* is *manmukh* according to SGGS:

ਦਿਤੈ ਕਿਤੈ ਨ ਸੰਤੋਖੀਅਹਿ ਅੰਤਰਿ ਤਿਸਨਾ ਬਹੁ ਅਗਿਆਨੁ ਅੰਧਾਰੁ ॥
Ditai kitai na santokhīah antar tisnā baho agiān andhyār.
No matter how much they receive, they are not content; their hearts are filled with dark
  and ignorant appetites.

ਨਾਨਕ ਮਨਮੁਖਾ ਨਾਲੋ ਤੁਟੀ ਭਲੀ ਜਿਨ ਮਾਇਆ ਮੋਹ ਪਿਆਰੁ ॥੧॥
Nānak manmukhā nālo tuṭī bhalī jin māiā moh piār. ||1||
Nanak, it is good to break away from those *manmukhā*, who are in love with
  attachment to *māiā.* ||1|| (316)

Here, *santokh* is explicitly contrasted with appetitive desire (*trisnā*) and attachment to the illusion of duality (*māiā moh)*. As discussed in relation to the vices, unrestrained appetitive desires are vicious because they reinforce duality between the self as subject and the objects of one's desires. Without *santokh*, the appetites grow out of control, manifesting as *kam, krodh*, and so on. *Santokh* is an antidote to the constant "I want … ", "I want …, " which reinforces the "I am me" of *haumai*. This is necessary for becoming *sachiār* – truthful to Oneness.

3.2.3 Sanjam

Sanjam is a virtue that is closely related to *santokh*, in that it has to do with keeping oneself from being ruled by one's appetites. It is usually translated as "temperance," but could also be translated as "discipline," "restraint," or "self-control." The concept of temperance will be familiar to Western philosophers, but parallels with Aristotelian conceptions should not be overstated.[29] *Sanjam* is neither in the first instance a form of moderation nor a mean between an excess and deficiency of appetite. Rather, it is the ability to control one's appetites instead of being controlled by them.

Another important clarification is that *sanjam* is not always used to refer to a virtue in SGGS. While *sanjam* often refers to the virtue of self-control, the same term can also refer to the kind of self-denial practiced by ascetics, which is rejected in Sikh ethics:

---

[29] See Avtar Singh (1970, 99) for an interesting discussion of the relationship between *sanjam* and
  Aristotelian temperance.

ਜਪੁ ਤਪ ਸੰਜਮ ਵਰਤ ਕਰੇ ਪੂਜਾ ਮਨਮੁਖ ਰੋਗੁ ਨ ਜਾਈ ॥

Jap tap sanjam varat kare pūjā manmukh rog na jāī.

The *manmukh* performs chants, fasts, and other rituals of self-denial, but their
  disease does not go away.

ਅੰਤਰਿ ਰੋਗੁ ਮਹਾ ਅਭਿਮਾਨਾ ਦੂਜੈ ਭਾਇ ਖੁਆਈ ॥੨॥

Antar rog mahā abhimānā dūjai bhāe khuāī. ||2||

The disease within is that of excessive self-regard; they are misled by love of
  duality. ||2|| (732)

Here, *sanjam* is used to describe the conduct of the *manmukh*, the vicious
person. When discussed in the context of ascetic practices such as ritual fasting,
sanjam refers to an austere self-denial that is seen as misguided and lacking in
virtue.

By contrast, when *sanjam* refers to the virtue of self-control, it is usually
explicitly connected to the idea of truthfulness by way of the phrases *sat sanjam*
or *sach sanjam – true* self-control, as opposed to the falsehood of ascetic self-
denial:

ਸਚੁ ਸੰਜਮੁ ਕਰਣੀ ਸੋ ਕਰੇ ਗੁਰਮੁਖਿ ਹੋਇ ਪਰਗਾਸੁ ॥੧॥ ਰਹਾਉ ॥

Sach sanjam karṇī so kare gurmukh hoe pargās. ||1|| rahāo.

Practicing deeds of true self-control, the *gurmukh* becomes enlightened. ||1||Pause|| (26)

A full explanation of why ascetic self-denial is false must wait until the
next section. The important point here is that when used as part of the
phrase *sach sanjam*, *sanjam* describes the *gurmukh*, the virtuous person.
The focus on true self-control as opposed to the falsehood of ascetic self-
denial brings out what the point of self-control is supposed to be in Sikh
ethics. The point is not to punish oneself for having appetites in order to
try to eradicate these appetites. The point, instead, is to be the master of
one's appetites. *Sanjam* refers to self-control in the sense of *self-mastery*
rather than self-denial.

In this way, *sanjam* and *santokh* are closely related. *Santokh* has to do with
not letting one's appetites multiply unchecked. The person without *santokh* is
never satisfied, always wanting more. *Sanjam* has to do with maintaining
control over the appetites one does have. Thus, both are about not being ruled
by appetitive desire (*trisnā*) and instead being ruled by truth. This is further
illuminated when they are discussed together:

ਸਤੁ ਸੰਤੋਖੁ ਸੰਜਮੁ ਹੈ ਨਾਲਿ ॥

Sat santokh sanjam hai nāl.

True contentment and self-control are your companions.

ਨਾਨਕ ਗੁਰਮੁਖਿ ਨਾਮੁ ਸਮਾਲਿ ॥੧੧॥
Nānak gurmukh nām samāl. ||11||
Nanak, the *gurmukh* contemplates the Divine Name. ||11|| (939)

In Sikh ethics, the problem with excessive appetitive desires is that they engross
one in duality, crowding out the Divine Name – *ik oaṅkār* – the Oneness of all.
For the *gurmukh*, both contentment and self-control are essential components of
truthfulness.

3.2.4 Saram

Saram can be translated as humility or modesty. Humility in SGGS is sometimes also referred to by the terms *maskīnī* and *garībī* (lit. poverty). All three of
these terms are used in context to refer to the trait that is contrary to the vice of
ahankār (arrogance). For example:

ਸੁਖੀ ਬਸੈ ਮਸਕੀਨੀਆ ਆਪੁ ਨਿਵਾਰਿ ਤਲੇ ॥
Sukhī basai maskīnīā āp nivār tale.
Those who are humble are filled with joy; they subdue self-regard from below.

ਬਡੇ ਬਡੇ ਅਹੰਕਾਰੀਆ ਨਾਨਕ ਗਰਬਿ ਗਲੇ ॥੧॥
Bade bade ahaṅkārīā Nānak garab gale. ||1||
Those of great arrogance, Nanak, are consumed by their own pride. ||1|| (278)

If arrogance consists in having excessive self-regard, then humility consists
in having appropriate self-regard. But what is an appropriate level of self-
regard can only be understood by reference to what it is to be *sachiār*. To be
sachiār is to be true to the ultimate reality of Oneness, in which there exists
no self-other duality. Though our experience is structured by this self-other
duality, we must understand its shallowness in order to become *sachiār*.

Those who are arrogant think they are better than others, and that they matter
more as a result. But the truth is that no one matters more than anyone else, and
any appearance as such is an illusion. Thus, those who are humble recognize
that we all matter in the same way, to the same degree, and so it is foolish to be
concerned with being above others. While the arrogant person, always concerned with their own status, is "consumed by their own pride," the humble
person "achieves bliss." Moreover, the humble person "subdues self-regard
from below." Only from the standpoint of recognizing their own flaws and not
estimating themselves too highly can self-regard be subdued. It cannot be
subdued from above, so to speak (hence the self-undermining nature of credit-
ing oneself with humility).

Humility (as *saram*) figures in multiple passages that are instructive for understanding the virtues in general, often in conjunction with *santokh*. In one, the ascetic is told:

ਮੁੰਦਾ ਸੰਤੋਖੁ ਸਰਮੁ ਪਤੁ ਝੋਲੀ ਧਿਆਨ ਕੀ ਕਰਹਿ ਬਿਭੂਤਿ ॥
Munda santokh saram pat jholī dhiān kī karahi bibhūt.
Make contentment your earrings, humility your begging bowl, and contemplation the ashes you apply to your body. (6)

Here the emphasis is on cultivating virtue rather than adorning oneself with the ascetic's outward signs of piety. In another passage, the cultivation of virtue is explained using the metaphor of farming:

ਮਨੁ ਹਾਲੀ ਕਿਰਸਾਣੀ ਕਰਣੀ ਸਰਮੁ ਪਾਣੀ ਤਨੁ ਖੇਤੁ ॥
Man hālī kirsāṇī karṇī saram pāṇī ṭan kheṭ.
Let your mind be the farmer, good deeds your farming, humility the water, and your body the field.

ਨਾਮੁ ਬੀਜੁ ਸੰਤੋਖੁ ਸੁਹਾਗਾ ਰਖੁ ਗਰੀਬੀ ਵੇਸੁ ॥
Nām bīj santokh suhāgā rakh garībī ves.
Let the Divine Name be the seed, contentment the plow, and humble dress the fence.

ਭਾਉ ਕਰਮ ਕਰਿ ਜੰਮਸੀ ਸੇ ਘਰ ਭਾਗਠ ਦੇਖੁ ॥੧॥
Bhāo karam kar jammsī se ghar bhāgaṭh ḍekh. ||1||
Acting out of love, the seed will sprout, and you will see your home flourish. ||1|| (595)[30]

In this metaphor, the mind is the farmer and the body is the field. The field of the body is farmed with good deeds, watered with humility, and plowed with contentment. This is instructive in part because it shows that virtues like humility and contentment are not solitary, inward-looking virtues. That is, one does not subdue *haumai* by renouncing the world and retreating to solitude. Instead, one accomplishes this through good deeds in the world.

3.2.5 Bibek

Bibek, in Sikh philosophy, is an aspect of wisdom (*giān*). Though wisdom in general is often listed by scholars as a particular virtue, I think it is too broad to function in this way. The wise person (*giānī* or *brahmgiānī*) is one who understands the whole truth of ultimate reality, not some particular aspect of it. Now, it might be thought that wisdom is still insufficient for truthfulness because it is an intellectual rather than a moral virtue. However,

---

[30] McLeod (1968, 222–223) claims that it is a mistake to interpret *saram* as humility here and instead interprets it as a Sanskrit-derived word meaning "effort." But McLeod's interpretation makes it difficult to make sense of other passages where *saram* is used, such as the previous one quoted, as well as why *saram* often appears alongside *santokh*.

this distinction cannot ultimately be sustained in Sikh philosophy. Because the truth cannot be fully apprehended without practicing it, there is no possibility of a truly wise person who apprehends the truth but does not practice it. Thus, I agree with Avtar Singh that "wisdom in Sikhism is considered to be inextricably linked with practice" (1966, 88). But what he does not realize is that this means that wisdom cannot be a particular virtue. If it requires practical in addition to intellectual understanding of the truth, then wisdom encapsulates all virtue and is nothing over and above truthfulness.

Bibek, on the other hand, is a particular virtue. It is standardly translated as discernment or discrimination. Self-examination, self-reflection, and self-awareness may also be helpful English terms. *Bibek* is considered a particularly important aspect of wisdom (and thus of virtue) in Sikh ethics because of the nature of *haumai* and our empirical existence in the world of self-other duality. Given that *haumai* is both the source of all vice and a natural condition of our existence as individuated selves, it is impossible for the virtuous person to completely eradicate *haumai*. To do so would be to permanently and irrevocably transcend one's consciousness as an individual self, which is not humanly possible. The virtuous person, by understanding and practicing Oneness, does not eradicate *haumai* but rather subdues it.[31]

The fact that *haumai* cannot be eradicated raises an epistemological challenge for the practice of Oneness. Given that *haumai* always resides within a person, even the *gurmukh*, how can anyone be sure they are not being influenced by *haumai*? Here lies the importance of *bibek*. The person with *bibek* is self-aware in the sense that they are able to discern the influence of *haumai*. Given that *haumai* is a kind of ignorance and falsehood, its nature is to disguise its own operation. This makes *bibek* crucial for virtue:

ਅੰਤਰਿ ਬਿਬੇਕੁ ਸਦਾ ਆਪੁ ਵੀਚਾਰੇ ਗੁਰ ਸਬਦੀ ਗੁਣ ਗਾਵਣਿਆ ॥੩॥

Antar bibek sadā āp vīchāre gur sabdī guṇ gāvaṇiā. ||3||

Those who have discernment continually examine their selves. Through
   the *sabad* of the *gurū*, they sing of the virtues. ||3|| (128)

This line is from a larger passage about subduing *haumai*. The message, in context, is that *haumai* can only be subdued if one has *bibek*. In other words, given the nature of *haumai*, one can only subdue it if one can discern it. This is why the virtuous person is described in SGGS as having a self-aware or

---

[31] According to Kaur (2025), references to reincarnation and the cycle of death and rebirth in Sikh philosophy are metaphors for the cycle of transcending and regressing back into *haumai*.

discerning intellect (*bibek budh*). Moreover, discernment is clearly a component of truthfulness, as one cannot be truthful without being able to discern truth from falsehood.

Given the focus in SGGS on how easy it is for us to fall into ignorance, illusion, and delusion, *bibek* seems to be a particularly important virtue. This is not to say that other aspects of wisdom are not important virtues in Sikh ethics. I have chosen to focus on it in part because it is importantly similar to the other virtues discussed. What *daiā, santokh, sanjam, saram,* and *bibek* have in common is that examining each of these virtues shows them to play distinct roles in subduing *haumai* so that we may become *sachiār* – truthful to Oneness. This does not entail that there are no other important virtues. It is just that these five are clearly identified in SGGS as particular aspects of the fundamental virtue of truthfulness.

3.3 Conclusion

I have presented an interpretation of vice and virtue in Sikh ethics on which each is unified. Vice is unified by *haumai,* which structures one's actions, thoughts, and feelings around a false conception of oneself as singularly important and fundamentally separate from others. The five thieves of *kām* (lust), *krodh* (wrath), *lobh* (greed), *moh* (attachment), and *ahankār* (arrogance) all manifest this tendency. Virtue is unified by truthfulness, which structures one's actions, thoughts, and feelings in ways that are true to the ultimate reality of Oneness. I have discussed how five important virtues, *daiā* (compassion), *santokh* (contentment), *sanjam* (self-control), *saram* (humility), and *bibek* (discernment), all manifest this tendency.

In discussing the particular vices and virtues, I have also tried to bring out the relationship between vice, virtue, and appetitive desire. Unchecked appetitive desires are considered a great danger in Sikh ethics. The more one is ruled by one's appetitive desires, the more one comes to see others as mere objects who exist for one's gratification. In this way, unchecked appetitive desires are closely related to *haumai* and the particular vices that manifest it. Correspondingly, the particular virtues are closely related to control over one's appetitive desires. It is a recurring theme in SGGS that one can only live truthfully if one's appetites (which present the world as structured by self-other duality) can be put in their place. But what kind of conduct does truthful living consist in? This is what I now turn to.

4 Right Conduct

So far, I have presented some of the foundational concepts of Sikh ethics and used them to reconstruct a systematic and unified theory of vice and virtue. The theory presented in the previous section is necessary for answering the central ethical question "How can one become truthful?" But it is not sufficient. To become truthful (*sachiār*), one must know what it is to be truthful. But knowing what it is to be truthful is not the same as knowing how to become truthful. The answer immediately given to the central ethical question in SGGS is that we become truthful by following *hukam* – the Divine Order of Oneness and the relation between all things. How do we follow *hukam*? That is the question of right conduct.

It is tempting to infer from the emphasis on becoming virtuous that Sikh ethics is a form of virtue ethics, where right conduct is a matter of doing what the virtuous person would do. It is true that in Sikh ethics, one ought to do as the truthful person would do, given that one ought to live truthfully. However, this does not entail a *priority* of virtue over right conduct. The more accurate interpretation of the relationship between virtue and right conduct in Sikh ethics is one on which neither is explained in terms of the other. Instead, each is explained in terms of more fundamental notions such as *hukam* and truthful living (*sach āchār*).

In general, we should be wary of assimilating Sikh ethics to some familiar Western system, such as virtue ethics, consequentialism, or deontology.[32] Yet it is equally important not to conclude that Sikh ethics lacks a systematic account of right and wrong. Despite the fact that SGGS is written in the form of scriptural poetry rather than treatise, it contains evaluative and deontic claims offering systematic guidance on what it is to follow *hukam* by living truthfully.

4.1 Karam

Evaluative and deontic claims in SGGS are often made using the words *karam* and *dharam*, respectively. Each of these terms can mean different things depending on the context, and are sometimes used purely descriptively, rather than in a normative sense. Western readers will likely associate *karam* with the idea of "karma" as a cosmic system of points one accrues through good or bad deeds. But this is usually not how *karam* is used in SGGS. Fundamentally, *karam* refers to action.[33] It can be used to describe actions in general; in such contexts it is a descriptive term. It can also be used in the familiar way to refer to a kind of accounting of one's past actions. But it is also often used evaluatively, to refer specifically to *good* actions or deeds. The same notion of good deeds can

---

[32] Garfield (2022, 18–20) astutely makes a similar point about Buddhist ethics.

[33] Garfield (2022, 14–15) makes a similar point about the use of the cognate term in Buddhist ethics. See also Bommarito (2020, Ch. 12).

also be referred to by synonyms such as *karṇī* (lit. to act, action). In all these cases, context determines the denotation of good deeds in particular as opposed to actions in general.

A final complication with the meaning of *karam* is that it can also be used to refer to actions that are not actually good but are merely considered good according to religion or culture. Because *karam*, when used this way, often refers to various religious rituals that are seen as good, it is standardly translated as "ritual" or "religious ritual" in this context. For example:

ਮਨਮੁਖ ਕਰਮ ਕਮਾਵਣੇ ਹਉਮੈ ਜਲੈ ਜਲਾਇ ॥

Manmukh karam kamāvṇe haumai jalai jalāe.
The *manmukh* perform religious rituals, yet they burn and burn in *haumai*. (68)

So, depending on the context, *karam* can refer simply to actions, to the sum of one's actions, to actions perceived as good, or to actions that are actually good. Only the fourth meaning is truly evaluative.

The contrast between *karam* as religious rituals and as truly good deeds is crucial in SGGS. This dual usage of *karam* is employed to criticize the prevailing notions of good action at the time and, by contrast, illustrate which actions are actually good according to Sikh ethics. In general, the comparison is drawn between rituals as outward displays of piety that are not done for the sake of others, and actions done for the sake of others. Such comparisons address both Hindu and Muslim rituals, as these were the dominant religious practices of the time and place. As reformers, the Sikh Gurus were generally critical of what they saw as a corruption of religion into hollow performances.

The following passage, for example, addresses Muslims, suggesting that praying five times a day is meaningless without good deeds:

ਪੰਜਿ ਨਿਵਾਜਾ ਵਖਤ ਪੰਜਿ ਪੰਜਾ ਪੰਜੇ ਨਾਉ ॥

Panj nivājā vakhat panj panjā panje nāo.
There are five prayers at five times of day; the five have five names.

ਪਹਿਲਾ ਸਚੁ ਹਲਾਲ ਦੁਇ ਤੀਜਾ ਖੈਰ ਖੁਦਾਇ ॥

Pahilā sach halāl due tījā khair khudāe.
Let the first be truthfulness, the second honest dealings, and the third Divine
generosity.[34]

ਚਉਥੀ ਨੀਅਤਿ ਰਾਸਿ ਮਨੁ ਪੰਜਵੀ ਸਿਫਤਿ ਸਨਾਇ ॥

Chauthī nīat rās man panjvī sifat sanāe.
Let the fourth be good intentions for all, and the fifth the praise of the Divine.

---

[34] In SGGS, Muslim names for the Divine are often used when addressing Muslims, and the names of Hindu deities are often used when addressing Hindus. This should not be mistaken for an expression of belief in a personal God or gods in the relevant passages.

ਕਰਣੀ ਕਲਮਾ ਆਖਿ ਕੈ ਤਾ ਮੁਸਲਮਾਣੁ ਸਦਾਇ ॥

Karṇī kalmā ākh kai tā musalmāṇ sadāe.

Make these good deeds your profession of faith, and then call yourself a Muslim.

ਨਾਨਕ ਜੇਤੇ ਕੂੜਿਆਰ ਕੂੜੈ ਕੂੜੀ ਪਾਇ ॥੩॥

Nānak jete kūṛiār kūṛhai kūṛī pāe. ||3||

Nanak, those who are false obtain only falsehood. ||3|| (141)

There are many such passages in SGGS, some addressing Muslims and some addressing various Hindu sects of the time. The message throughout all of them is that religious rituals, regardless of their intended function, had become outward performances of piety. Such performances are false, and through them one obtains only falsehood. Instead, the true good deeds are identified with truthful living, honest dealings, charitable giving, and so on.

Part of the point of such passages is to criticize social norms that uphold actions as good even when they are performed out of narrow self-interest. Any attempt at personal piety that is purely self-regarding can only be an instance of *haumai*. *Karam* in the sense of good deeds, then, can generally be understood as picking out those actions that positively affect those other than the agent. However, even the performance of deeds that are good in this sense is not sufficient for right conduct. It is important not just how one's actions affect others but also how they are motivated:

ਅਹੰਬੁਧਿ ਕਰਮ ਕਮਾਵਨੇ ॥

Aha'nbudh karam kamāvane.

Good deeds done pridefully

ਗ੍ਰਿਹ ਬਾਲੂ ਨੀਰਿ ਬਹਾਵਨੇ ॥੩॥

Grih bālū nīr bahāvane. ||3||

are swept away like a sandcastle by water. ||3|| (211)

The point here is not that selfishly motivated actions are valueless. They are still good deeds in the sense that they benefit others. But the goodness of these deeds, while necessary, is insufficient for right conduct. On the Sikh conception of right conduct, it must also be motivated in the right way.

One clearly expressed condition on right conduct in Sikh ethics is that it must not be done for the sake of reward, or any other ulterior motive:

ਬੈਸਨੋ ਸੋ ਜਿਸੁ ਊਪਰਿ ਸੁਪ੍ਰਸੰਨ ॥

Baisno so jis ūpar suparsan.

The Vaishnav who truly pleases the Divine

ਬਿਸਨ ਕੀ ਮਾਇਆ ਤੇ ਹੋਇ ਭਿੰਨ ॥
Bisan kī māiā te hoe bhinn.
lives apart from the *māiā* of Vishnu.

ਕਰਮ ਕਰਤ ਹੋਵੈ ਨਿਹਕਰਮ ॥
Karam karat hovai nihkaram.
He performs good deeds without desire for reward.

ਤਿਸੁ ਬੈਸਨੋ ਕਾ ਨਿਰਮਲ ਧਰਮ ॥
Tis baisno kā nirmal dharam.
This Vaishnav's *dharam* is pure.

ਕਾਹੂ ਫਲ ਕੀ ਇਛਾ ਨਹੀ ਬਾਛੈ ॥
Kāhū phal kī ichhā nahī bāchhai.
He has no desire for the fruits of his labors. (274)

This passage addresses the Vaishnavite Hindu. It again sets up a contrast with someone who practices religious rituals selfishly, out of a desire for reward from their God. Such a desire is identified as *māiā* – illusion. But the one who performs good deeds unselfishly, and has no ulterior motive of personal benefit, is described as having *nirmal dharam* – pure right conduct. Thus, though *karam* is important, it is insufficient for right conduct. Right conduct in Sikh ethics is determined not just by effects but also by motive. Hence, Sikh ethics cannot be seen as a form of consequentialism.

4.2 Dharam

This brings us to further explication of the notion of *dharam* in Sikh ethics. Like *karam*, *dharam* can be used descriptively or normatively. Sometimes, in its purely descriptive usage, it refers to religiosity, or to the kind of conduct held up as right by various religious rules. In other contexts, it refers to the properly deontic concept of right conduct. *Dharam* in its deontic usage is often translated as "duty." However, *dharam* applies not just to right action but also to right thought and feeling. *Dharam* in its deontic usage is meant to cover all of how we choose to conduct ourselves – hence, "right conduct" is a better translation.

The contrast between the descriptive and deontic usages of *dharam* functions similarly to the contrast between the descriptive and evaluative usages of *karam* discussed above. Just as religious rituals seen as good are contrasted with truly good deeds in SGGS, the deliverances of religious edicts are contrasted with true rightness of conduct. For example, here both *karam* and dharam are used descriptively:

ਕਰਮ ਧਰਮ ਕਰਤੇ ਬਹੁ ਸੰਜਮ ਅਹੰਬੁਧਿ ਮਨੁ ਜਾਰਿਓ ਰੇ ॥੧॥

Karam dharam karte baho sanjam aha'nbudh man jārio re. ||1||

They practice religious rituals, follow religious edicts, and many forms of self-denial, yet their minds are consumed by pride. ||1|| (335)[35]

Again, the message is criticism of what is uncritically accepted as right conduct. A person could be pious in all the ways prescribed by their religion, but still their conduct is not right if their minds are consumed by pride.

Compare the above passage with the following, where *karam* and *dharam* are used normatively:

ਕਰਮ ਧਰਮ ਤੁਮ੍ ਚਉਪੜਿ ਸਾਜਹੁ ਸਤੁ ਕਰਹੁ ਤੁਮ੍ ਸਾਰੀ ॥

Karam dharam tumh chaupaṛ sājahu sat karahu tumh sārī.

Let good deeds and right conduct be your game board, and let truth be your game pieces.

ਕਾਮੁ ਕ੍ਰੋਧੁ ਲੋਭੁ ਮੋਹੁ ਜੀਤਹੁ ਐਸੀ ਖੇਲ ਹਰਿ ਪਿਆਰੀ ॥੨॥

Kām krodh lobh moh jītahu aisī khel har piārī. ||2||

Conquer lust, wrath, greed and attachment; such a game is the love of the Divine. ||2|| (1185)

It is clear from context here that *karam* and *dharam* refer to what are truly good actions and right conduct, rather than that which is merely seen as such by social or religious norms. In the metaphor, right conduct is the game board and truth is the game piece. This means that the true *dharam* is, at root, truthful living (*sach āchār*) itself. And here, truthful living is identified with the love of the Divine (of which everyone and everything is a manifestation).

So far, we have seen that Sikh ethics rejects any identification of right conduct with unquestioning adherence to religious edicts. Such acts of personal piety are largely seen as selfishly motivated attempts to gain some benefit, whether worldly or spiritual, and thus as without any moral merit. The only true *dharam* is to live truthfully. From what has been presented about vice and virtue, we have plenty of clues as to what living truthfully entails. To live truthfully is to be true to Oneness, which means not just appreciating the unity of ultimate reality but *practicing* it. This involves subduing *haumai* and the corresponding five thieves, and exerting control over one's appetites. It involves caring for others as one cares for oneself. But more can be said here if we further examine what SGGS says about how to treat others.

It is an important part of the idea of truthful living in Sikh ethics that it cannot be achieved purely through intellectual apprehension, or through any solitary spiritual practice (recall the discussion in the previous section of why there

---

[35] Here, *sanjam* is used not to refer to the virtue of self-control but to self-denial, as distinguished in the discussion of *sanjam* in Section 2.

cannot be purely intellectual virtues). One can try all one wants to connect with Oneness in these ways, but it will be futile:

ਜਹ ਕਰਣੀ ਤਹ ਪੂਰੀ ਮਤਿ ॥
Jah karṇī tah pūrī mat.
Through good deeds, one's understanding [of the Divine] is completed.

ਕਰਣੀ ਬਾਝਹੁ ਘਟੇ ਘਟਿ ॥੩॥
Karṇī bājhahu ghate ghat. ||3||
Without good deeds, it lessens and lessens. ||3|| (25)

It is part of the nature of the Divine that acquaintance with it is an ethical matter rather than a purely intellectual one.

In addition to contemplating the Divine, one must acquaint oneself with it by acquainting oneself with the whole of reality. From a Sikh philosophical perspective, everyone is a part of a whole that has been separated from that whole through being embodied as an individually conscious self. Without acquainting oneself with the true nature of others by treating them as manifestations of that very same Oneness, one cannot be truthful to ultimate reality. This is what I refer to as "practicing Oneness." This way of orienting oneself toward others is described in SGGS as recognizing the "Divine Light" (*jot*) in everyone:

ਗੁਰਮੁਖਿ ਏਕ ਦ੍ਰਿਸਟਿ ਕਰਿ ਦੇਖਹੁ ਘਟਿ ਘਟਿ ਜੋਤਿ ਸਮੋਈ ਜੀਉ ॥੨॥
Gurmukh ek darisat kar dekhhu ghat ghat jot samoī jīo. ||2||
As *gurmukh*, look upon all with equality; the Divine Light resides in
    everyone. ||2|| (599)

Oneness is practiced by treating all people as having equal worth. This sort of universality may seem commonplace in ethical theory now, but it was radical at the time. The ethics presented in SGGS were developed in a context of extreme hierarchy, as exemplified by the rigid caste system that was followed in South Asia. Moreover, the emphasis on universality and equality in Sikh ethics was radical not just by the standards of South Asia but globally, as it precedes such emphasis in European philosophy by a significant margin.

Against the hierarchical and inegalitarian social norms of the day, the message of SGGS is that caste is a delusion, part of *māiā*, that must be seen through in order to live truthfully:

ਜਾਣਹੁ ਜੋਤਿ ਨ ਪੂਛਹੁ ਜਾਤੀ ਆਗੈ ਜਾਤਿ ਨ ਹੇ ॥੧॥ ਰਹਾਉ ॥
Jāṇhu jot na pūchhahu jātī āgai jāt na he. ||1|| rahāo.
Recognize the Divine Light within all, and do not consider caste; there are no castes
    in the next world. ||1||Pause|| (349)

As I interpret it, "the next world" refers not to a literal afterlife but to the world of ultimate reality. The point is that all social hierarchies are constructions of the world of ordinary conscious experience, a world structured by self-other duality. These social hierarchies are shown to be illusory at the level of ultimate reality. So, to grasp the ultimate reality of Oneness, we must eschew distinctions of caste and social hierarchy. Any attachment to caste or social hierarchy is borne out of *haumai* and thus constitutes a false way of living.

The above understanding of practicing Oneness places another constraint on the intentions or motives required for right conduct. Just as right conduct cannot be motivated by selfish concerns, it also cannot be motivated by parochial concerns, including concern for one's own caste, race, gender, religion, etc. In-group bias and the construction of hierarchies based on social identity are antithetical to the practice of Oneness and thus to Sikh *dharam*. In addition to the above passages from SGGS, the importance of being motivated by universal concern is illustrated by an event from Sikh history which has become an important part of Sikh moral consciousness and moral education. The story concerns Bhai Kanhaiya, a follower of Guru Gobind Singh. In the aftermath of a battle against Mughal forces, Bhai Kanhaiya was seen giving water not just to the injured Sikh soldiers but also to the Mughals. When questioned about this practice, Bhai Kanhaiya famously replied that he saw no Sikh or Mughal on the battlefield, only people.

This story illustrates that truly right conduct is not just a matter of the external features of one's actions but also a matter of the orientation toward the world they reflect. Bhai Kanhaiya's conduct is held up as exemplary in Sikh moral consciousness precisely because, as the story goes, he literally could not see the differences between his side and another. All he saw were people in need, and he was directly moved to help without considering any divisions between them. In this way, right conduct in Sikh ethics is a mode of thought and feeling, not just action. To conduct oneself rightly is to transcend the shallow divisions created by individuated subjectivity and thereby to transcend *haumai*. *Dharam* in Sikh ethics is to see rightly, think rightly, feel rightly, and act rightly, practicing Oneness in all facets of one's conduct.

4.3 Sahaj

In light of the above, it becomes clear that right conduct in Sikh ethics is enabled by a particular mode of consciousness, from which one is able to see, think, feel, and act rightly. This mode of consciousness is called *sahaj*, an important concept in Sikh philosophy that is difficult to translate faithfully into English. It has been translated variously as balance, poise, easefulness, peace, spontaneity, and intuition.[36] More precisely, *sahaj* refers to the state of being in which one has quelled the mental chaos of *haumai* and *trisnā* (appetitive desire) so that one can approach one's conduct with clarity of consciousness:

ਸਤਿਗੁਰੁ ਸੇਵਿਐ ਸਹਜੁ ਉਪਜੈ ਹਉਮੈ ਤ੍ਰਿਸਨਾ ਮਾਰਿ ॥
Satgur seviai sahj ūpjai haumai trisnā mār.
Serving the True *gurū*, one achieves *sahaj* as one subdues *haumai* and appetitive
  desire.

ਹਰਿ ਗੁਣਦਾਤਾ ਸਦ ਮਨਿ ਵਸੈ ਸਚੁ ਰਖਿਆ ਉਰ ਧਾਰਿ ॥੬॥
Har guṇdātā sad man vasai sach rakhiā ur dhār. ||6||
The Divine bestower of virtue resides in minds of those who practice Truth in their
  hearts. ||6|| (65)

As this passage tells us, *sahaj* is seen as the mode of consciousness that enables us to achieve virtue by living truthfully. *Sahaj* enables truthful living because it is a state in which *haumai* and appetitive desire have been subdued.

Sahaj is also the mode of consciousness in which we are able to see through duality, which is necessary for truthful living:

ਸਹਜੇ ਹਰਿ ਨਾਮੁ ਮਨਿ ਵਸਿਆ ਸਚੀ ਕਾਰ ਕਮਾਇ ॥
Sėhje har nām man vasiā sachī kār kamāe.
In *sahaj*, the the Divine Name dwells in one's mind; one practices truthful living.

ਸੇ ਵਡਭਾਗੀ ਜਿਨੀ ਪਾਇਆ ਸਹਜੇ ਰਹੇ ਸਮਾਇ ॥੪॥
Se vadbhāgī jinī pāiā sėhje rahe samāe. ||4||
Those who have found [the Divine] are very fortunate; in *sahaj*, they remain absorbed
  in it. ||4||

ਮਾਇਆ ਵਿਚਿ ਸਹਜੁ ਨ ਉਪਜੈ ਮਾਇਆ ਦੂਜੈ ਭਾਇ ॥
Māiā vich sahj na ūpjai māiā dūjai bhāe.
Within *māiā*, *sahaj* is not produced; *māiā* leads to the love of duality. (68)

The illusion (*māiā*) of deep self-other duality produces attachment to this duality. As we have seen, this dualistic mode of consciousness is the home of *haumai* and unrestrained appetites. This is a tortured state, as one constantly experiences one's own lack of gratification as privation. By contrast, when one has subdued *haumai* and appetitive desire, one is able to see clearly, thereby achieving a state of peace and poise (hence some of the common translations). It is claimed throughout SGGS that when one achieves the mode of consciousness that enables one to see through duality to the Oneness of all, one finally finds

---

[36] Kaur (2025, 64–65) helpfully describes *sahaj* as an "easeful mode of becoming," and the mode
  of being "effortlessly in rhythm with hukam."

respite from the self-torture of one's *haumai* and appetitive desires.[37] It is in this state of *sahaj* that one is most able to conduct oneself in ways that are truthful to this Oneness.

Sahaj is also explicitly connected to *karam* and *dharam* in SGGS, making clear its role as an enabling condition of good deeds and right conduct:

ਸਹਜੇ ਜਾ ਕਉ ਪਰਿਓ ਕਰਮਾ ॥
Sèhje jā kao pario karmā.
In *sahaj*, they [the *gurmukh*] perform good deeds.

ਸਹਜੇ ਗੁਰੁ ਭੇਟਿਓ ਸਚੁ ਧਰਮਾ ॥
Sèhje gur bhetio sach dharmā.
In *sahaj*, they meet the *gurū* with true *dharam*. (237)

Sahaj is also highlighted as the mode of consciousness in which the Divine Light can be recognized:

ਜੋਤਿ ਨਿਰੰਤਰਿ ਜਾਣੀਐ ਨਾਨਕ ਸਹਜਿ ਸੁਭਾਇ ॥੮॥੩॥
Jot nirantar jāṇīai Nānak sahj subhāe. ||8||3||
The Divine Light within all is recognized, Nanak, through achieving *sahaj*. ||8||3|| (55)

As explained in the previous section, the "Divine Light" (*jot*) is referred to in SGGS as residing in everyone, with the implication that everyone should be treated with equality, and that social hierarchies of caste, etc., are irrelevant to a person's worth. Taken together, the above passages regarding *sahaj* paint a systematic guide to right conduct. Right conduct is truthful living. Truthful living is the practice of Oneness. The practice of Oneness is the practice of universal, egalitarian concern for everyone. This practice requires subduing one's self-centered and parochial desires, and entering a mode of consciousness where one is able to conduct oneself with this universal, egalitarian concern.

Attending to the role of *sahaj* in Sikh ethics also helps to bring out why neither of virtue or right conduct is explanatorily prior to the other. *Sahaj* is the mode of consciousness that enables right conduct, but it is itself facilitated by virtuous character traits that have to do with subduing *haumai*. Yet, a person who is not a *gurmukh* (virtuous person) can still act rightly, even if they have no stable disposition to do so, and their acting rightly need not be understood in terms of acting as the virtuous person would. Instead, one-off instances of right conduct can be explained in terms of a fleeting achievement of *sahaj* – the mode of consciousness in which the agent is able to apprehend and practice Oneness.

---

[37] Relatedly, Dewan Singh (2001, 73) connects *sahaj* to "the acceptance of *Hukam*."

4.4 Householder and Renunciate

Many central concepts of Sikh ethics have to do with subduing and exerting control over one's appetitive desires. It might naturally be thought, then, that Sikh ethics idealizes the renunciate: someone who has given up worldly pursuits to pursue enlightenment and connect with the Divine. But this is not quite right. In fact, the ascetic lifestyle is repeatedly (and sometimes stridently) criticized as self-indulgent and self-defeating throughout SGGS. In considering right conduct in Sikh ethics, it is instructive to consider why, and what relationship we ought to have to worldly pursuits if not renunciation.

Bits and pieces of the answers to these questions have already been presented. In this section and the previous one, we have already seen passages from SGGS that criticize ascetics for their misguided approach. One such passage criticized fasts and other rituals of self-denial as doing nothing to cure them of their love of duality. Other passages emphasize that the various external performances of piety practiced by ascetic sects are useless for achieving enlightenment, and that they should instead make good deeds and service to others their accoutrements. A fuller understanding of these criticisms will help illuminate why complete self-denial and eschewal of worldly pursuits are self-indulgent and self-defeating.

It is repeatedly made clear in SGGS that no amount of solitary contemplation or spiritual practice can connect one with the Divine:

ਕਬਿਤ ਪੜੇ ਪੜਿ ਕਬਿਤਾ ਮੂਏ ਕਪੜ ਕੇਦਾਰੈ ਜਾਈ ॥

Kabit pare par kabitā mūe kapar kedārai jāī.
Reciting their poems, the poets die; the ascetics die journeying to Kedarnath.[38]

ਜਟਾ ਧਾਰਿ ਧਾਰਿ ਜੋਗੀ ਮੂਏ ਤੇਰੀ ਗਤਿ ਇਨਹਿ ਨ ਪਾਈ ॥੨॥

Jatā dhār dhār jogī mūe terī gat ineh na pāī. ||2||
The Yogis die with matted hair; even then, they do not find Your nature. ||2|| (654)

This and many other passages criticize ascetics for performing rituals and pilgrimages that are ultimately meaningless. Practices of self-mortification, ritual bathing, and so on, which are meant to annihilate the self, or somehow transcend the flesh, are the subject of similarly harsh condemnation throughout SGGS. In fact, it is explicitly stated that such rituals do nothing to address the problem of *haumai*:

ਮਲੁ ਹਉਮੈ ਧੋਤੀ ਕਿਵੈ ਨ ਉਤਰੈ ਜੇ ਸਉ ਤੀਰਥ ਨਾਇ ॥

Mal haumai dhotī kivai na utrai je sao tirath nāe.
The filth of *haumai* cannot be removed by washing, even by bathing at
a hundred sacred shrines.

---

[38] A Hindu temple and pilgrimage site.

ਬਹੁ ਬਿਧਿ ਕਰਮ ਕਮਾਵਦੇ ਦੂਣੀ ਮਲੁ ਲਾਗੀ ਆਇ ॥

Baho bidh karam kamāvde dūṇī mal lāgī āe.

Performing all sorts of rituals, twice as much filth sticks to them. (39)

According to this passage, not only does the performance of such rituals fail to subdue *haumai*, it actually makes it worse.

By renouncing the world in order to find the Divine, these renunciates show that they lack understanding of its nature. If the Divine is the ultimate reality that unifies everything, then withdrawing from the rest of the world to search for ultimate reality is futile. If these renunciates truly knew the Divine, then they would care about other people as fellow constituents of Divine Oneness. Instead, they care only for themselves and their self-centered quest for enlightenment. Through self-indulgent attempts to cleanse and mortify themselves, these renunciates continue to act in a self-regarding, inward-facing manner. They are, quite literally, *manmukh*.[39]

By contrast, the *gurmukh* makes the performance of good deeds their ritual:

ਗੁਰਮੁਖਿ ਮਜਨੁ ਚਜੁ ਅਚਾਰੁ ॥

Gurmukh majan chaj achār.

The *gurmukh's* ablution is the performance of good deeds. (932)

The way one cleanses oneself of *haumai*, and thereby becomes virtuous, is through the performance of good deeds. Moreover, as we have already seen, these good deeds must be performed selflessly for them to rise to the level of right conduct. Thus, both right conduct and virtue must be achieved through living in the world with others, not through renunciation.

By contrast to the renunciate (*udāsā*), many verses of SGGS hold up the householder (*girhī*) as an ideal:

ਇਕਿ ਤਪਸੀ ਬਨ ਮਹਿ ਤਪੁ ਕਰਹਿ ਨਿਤ ਤੀਰਥ ਵਾਸਾ ॥

Ik tapsī ban mėh tap karahi nit tirath vāsā.

Some ascetics perform penance in the forests, and some reside forever at sacred shrines.

ਆਪੁ ਨ ਚੀਨਹਿ ਤਾਮਸੀ ਕਾਹੇ ਭਏ ਉਦਾਸਾ ॥੫॥

Āp na chīnėh tāmsī kāhe bhae udāsā. ||5||

They do not understand themselves – why have they become renunciates? ||5||

ਇਕਿ ਬਿੰਦੁ ਜਤਨ ਕਰਿ ਰਾਖਦੇ ਸੇ ਜਤੀ ਕਹਾਵਹਿ ॥

Ik bind jatan kar rākhde se jatī kahāvėh.

Some practice sexual denial and are known as celibates.

---

[39] Kapur Singh (1991, 107) similarly points out the futility of ascetic self-annihilation from the Sikh perspective.

ਬਿਨੁ ਗੁਰ ਸਬਦ ਨ ਛੁਟਹੀ ਭ੍ਰਮਿ ਆਵਹਿ ਜਾਵਹਿ ॥੬॥

Bin gur sabad na chhūṭhī bhram āvahi jāvėh. ||6||

But without the Guru's word, they wander in ignorance. ||6||

ਇਕਿ ਗਿਰਹੀ ਸੇਵਕ ਸਾਧਿਕਾ ਗੁਰਮਤੀ ਲਾਗੇ ॥

Ik girhī sevak sādhikā gurmatī lāge.

Some are householders, serve others, and engage in worldly pursuits, within the
   gurū's wisdom.

ਨਾਮੁ ਦਾਨੁ ਇਸਨਾਨੁ ਦ੍ਰਿੜੁ ਹਰਿ ਭਗਤਿ ਸੁ ਜਾਗੇ ॥੭॥

Nām dān isnān driṛ har bhagat so jāge. ||7||

Practicing contemplation of the Divine Name, beneficence, and purity of conduct,
   they are awake in devotion. ||7|| (419)

According to the above passage, there is a way of being a householder that is
"within the *gurū*'s wisdom." This involves practicing *nām dān isnān*, a trio of
pillars of conduct invoked several times in SGGS. *Nām* refers to contemplation
of the Divine Name, which can take the form of recitation of scripture and
singing of sacred songs. *Dān* refers to beneficence (especially the sharing of
resources), and *isnān* refers to purity of conduct.

Purity has to do with negative duties – what one must refrain from doing.
Isnān (lit. cleansing) involves refraining from those actions that are done out of
haumai.[40] By contrast, beneficence is a paradigmatic *positive duty* – it must be
fulfilled by taking action, not just refraining from certain conduct. *Dān* involves
acting in ways that reflect the Oneness of all through doing good deeds for
others. The injunction to practice *dān* and not just *isnān* shows that one must
engage in worldly actions despite the risk this poses to the control of one's
appetites. One must learn to live in the world while subduing *haumai*; to
renounce the world is, in short, a cop out.

Though *nām* may seem solitary in contrast to *dān* and *isnān*, it too has a social
component. Since its inception, a crucial part of Sikh practice has been contemplation of the Divine Name in community (*sādh sangat*). Reciting scripture
(*nām simran*), singing sacred songs (*sabad kīrtan*), engaging in philosophical
discourse (*kathā*), and communal dining (*langar*) are all to be done in community. This collective and communal aspect of *nām* is seen as having great ethical
importance. As Inderjit Kaur puts it:

---

[40] The concept of *isnān* reappropriates the standards of purity and pollution from the unethical caste
     system it so heavily criticizes. In contrast to the caste system, in which those of high caste would
     perform ablutions to "purify" themselves from the "pollution" of coming into contact with those
     of low caste, Sikh ethics tells us that the only true pollution is that of *haumai*, and the only true
     purification is conquering *haumai*.

> For Sikhs, the paired rituals of open- house *sabad kīrtan* (collective singing,
> pronounced "*keertan*") and *langar* (communal dining) negate social hierarch-
> ies and exclusion; this practice of regularly transcending social boundaries
> (particularly caste and class) aims to habituate equal treatment of all human
> beings." (2024, 229)

Kaur emphasizes that the root of these ethical obligations in Sikhism is the
ultimate unity or Oneness of all. So, even the practice of *nām* is incompatible
with renunciation.

Right conduct in Sikh ethics, then, requires living in this world of *haumai* and
duality, but while also trying to transcend those features of it, which itself can
only be done by living in this world. Any attempt to transcend *haumai* through
ascetic practices is self-defeating, because the attempt to achieve enlightenment
through self-annihilation is just another form of self-indulgence. Though there
is a sense in which one ought to renounce *haumai* and attachment to duality, this
cannot take the form of renouncing the world and worldly pursuits without
itself becoming a form of *haumai*. This makes sense of passages in SGGS that
may be otherwise perplexing. For example, it is at one point said of wandering
ascetics:

ਬਿਰਥਾ ਜਨਮੁ ਗਵਾਇ ਨ ਗਿਰਹੀ ਨ ਉਦਾਸਾ ॥
Birthā janam gavāe na girhī na udāsā.
They waste their lives away in vain; they are neither householders nor
    renunciates. (140)

By contrast:

ਕਹੁ ਨਾਨਕ ਗੁਰੁ ਪੂਰਾ ਭੇਟਿਆ ਪਰਵਾਣੁ ਗਿਰਸਤ ਉਦਾਸ ॥੪॥੪॥੫॥
Kaho Nānak gur pūrā bheṭiā parvāṇ girsat udās. ||4||4||5||
Says Nanak, one who meets the perfect *gurū* is both householder and
    renunciate. ||4||4||5|| (496)

These passages seem to contradict the earlier description of ascetics as renunciates *as opposed to* householders, and of the virtuous as householders *as opposed
to* renunciates. Moreover, the second passage seems to ascribe the contraries of
householder and renunciate to the same person.

How can someone be both householder and renunciate? The answer is that
the *gurmukh* is both householder in the sense that they participate in worldly
pursuits and renunciate in the sense that they renounce *haumai* and attachment
to duality. But the *gurmukh* does not renounce the world as the ascetic does. The
ascetic is not a householder because they renounce worldly pursuits but also not
a renunciate in the positive sense, because they are still filled with *haumai* and
attached to duality.

Still, one might still wonder to what degree this notion of a householder permits one to engage in worldly pursuits. One might point to the injunction to be a householder as justification for accumulating substantial wealth and personal possessions. But I do not think this can be justified by what is said in SGGS. Of course, being a householder must be compatible with possessing some amount of personal property. A modestly comfortable life, unlike the self-denial of the ascetic, does not seem incompatible with subduing *haumai* and practicing Oneness. But the accumulation of vast wealth and property, especially at the expense of others who are suffering, does seem incompatible with truthful living.

In an instructive passage, Guru Nanak addresses a hypothetical "merchant friend" who is focused on the accumulation of wealth and vain pursuits:

ਤੀਜੈ ਪਹਰੈ ਰੈਣਿ ਕੈ ਵਣਜਾਰਿਆ ਮਿਤ੍ਰਾ ਧਨ ਜੋਬਨ ਸਿਉ ਚਿਤੁ ॥
Tijai pahrai raiṇ kai vaṇjāriā mitrā dhan joban sio chit.
In the third watch of the night, merchant friend, your consciousness is oriented toward
     wealth and youth.

ਹਰਿ ਕਾ ਨਾਮੁ ਨ ਚੇਤਹੀ ਵਣਜਾਰਿਆ ਮਿਤ੍ਰਾ ਬਧਾ ਛੁਟਹਿ ਜਿਤੁ ॥
Har kā nām na chethī vaṇjāriā mitrā badhā chhutèh jit.
You have not contemplated the Divine Name, merchant friend, though it would free you
     from your bonds.

ਹਰਿ ਕਾ ਨਾਮੁ ਨ ਚੇਤੈ ਪ੍ਰਾਣੀ ਬਿਕਲੁ ਭਇਆ ਸੰਗਿ ਮਾਇਆ ॥
Har kā nām na chetai prāṇī bikal bhaiā sang māiā.
You do not contemplate the Divine Name; you are stupefied by *māiā*.

ਧਨ ਸਿਉ ਰਤਾ ਜੋਬਨਿ ਮਤਾ ਅਹਿਲਾ ਜਨਮੁ ਗਵਾਇਆ ॥
Dhan sio ratā joban matā ahilā janam gavāiā.
Intoxicated by wealth and youth, you waste your life away in vain.

ਧਰਮ ਸੇਤੀ ਵਾਪਾਰੁ ਨ ਕੀਤੋ ਕਰਮੁ ਨ ਕੀਤੋ ਮਿਤੁ ॥
Dharam setī vāpār na kīto karam na kīto mit.
You have not made *dharam* your business, nor have you made *karam* your friend.

ਕਹੁ ਨਾਨਕ ਤੀਜੈ ਪਹਰੈ ਪ੍ਰਾਣੀ ਧਨ ਜੋਬਨ ਸਿਉ ਚਿਤੁ ॥੩॥
Kaho Nānak tījai pahrai parāṇī dhan joban sio chit. ||3||
Says Nanak, in the third watch, your consciousness is oriented towards wealth and
     youth. ||3|| (75)

In SGGS, the four watches of the night are metaphors for stages of life, with the third representing the bulk of adulthood, before old age. Here, the merchant friend is told that his focus on "wealth and youth" leaves him stupefied by *māiā*. Moreover, this has prevented him from focusing adequately on right conduct and the performance of good deeds. Right conduct, as the practice of Oneness, is described throughout SGGS as the "true business" (*sachā saudā*), in contrast to the accumulation of wealth and property:

ਸਚਾ ਸਉਦਾ ਹਰਿ ਨਾਮੁ ਹੈ ਸਚਾ ਵਾਪਾਰਾ ਰਾਮ ॥
Sachā saudā har nām hai sachā vāpārā rām.
The true business is the Divine Name, and the Divine is the true trade.

I conclude that the conception of right conduct in Sikh ethics puts significant limits on the degree to which wealth and property may be pursued. In particular, any accumulation of wealth and property that is incompatible with others having enough can only enforce self-other duality and can only express the view that oneself is more important than others. Thus, even though a Sikh is enjoined to be a householder, they must live modestly and are not to go beyond what is necessary for a comfortable life, especially while others are suffering. If society is set up so that some people accumulate too much, it is made clear in SGGS that their duty is to give it away or otherwise use it to benefit others.

4.5 Conclusion

I have presented an interpretation of right conduct in Sikh ethics on which it is to be understood in terms of truthful living. In the previous section, I argued that virtue in Sikh ethics is to be understood in terms of truthfulness. This shows how virtue and right conduct are integrated. Instead of explaining either of virtue or right conduct in terms of the other, Sikh ethics explains both in terms of the fundamental importance of living in ways that reflect the ultimate reality of Oneness.

As I have explained, right conduct in Sikh ethics is not just about what one does but how one does it. Moreover, it is not just about action but also thought and feeling. To conduct oneself rightly, one's actions must reflect the equal worth of everyone not just in their outward manifestation but also in the thoughts and feelings that motivate them. This is why right action *par excellence* requires achieving *sahaj* – the mode of consciousness in which one is able to see through duality to the Oneness of all.

Finally, I have explained how right conduct in Sikh ethics requires striking a balance between living as householder and renunciate. Those who are focused on the accumulation of wealth and personal property fail to practice Oneness because they are motivated by their appetites, which are self-regarding and reinforce self-other duality. But those who attempt to achieve enlightenment through self-denial and self-mortification also fail to practice Oneness. By ignoring the importance of others, their conduct is equally self-regarding and reinforcing of self-other duality. Only those who are able to live in the world while fully recognizing the significance of others are able to transcend self-other duality and conduct themselves rightly.

5 Sikh Ethics in Practice

So far, my reconstruction of Sikh ethics has focused on the primary text of Sikh scripture. I have tried to show that there is a coherent and systematic ethical theory whose essential features are fully contained within SGGS. That it requires reconstruction to be understood does not impugn the status of this theory. After all, all such systematic theorizing in the history of philosophy requires reconstruction in order to elucidate how a coherent system is presented. The need for these features to be drawn out and explained through close textual analysis should no more be seen as a problem for Sikh ethics than it is for any other system of ethics.

In this final section, I explore central Sikh ethical practices that have developed since the enshrinement of SGGS as scripture. In particular, my goal is to show how these ethical practices function as extensions and applications of the ethical theory found in SGGS. In doing so, I put philosophical pressure on an interpretation, popular in the field of Sikh Studies, on which Sikh practices post-SGGS are reformatory of, or otherwise discontinuous with, the philosophy presented in SGGS.

I focus on the *panj kakār* (five Ks), the three pillars of conduct (*nām japnā, kirat karnī, vaṇḍ chhaknā*), and the congregational practices of *sabad kirtan* (collective singing) and *langar* (communal dining). I endeavor to explain how, with the Sikh ethical theory presented in the previous sections in view, all of these practices can be interpreted as extensions and applications of that theory. Thus, I argue, these Sikh practices remain fully continuous and coherent with the philosophical message of SGGS.

5.1 Panj Kakār

The *panj kakār*, or five Ks, so named because they all begin with the letter K, are arguably the most significant development in the institutionalization of Sikh practice post-SGGS. They are *kes* (uncut hair), *kanghā* (comb), *kaṛā* (steel bracelet), *kachherā* (undershorts), and *kirpan* (sword or dagger). According to Sikh communal history, the five Ks were instituted by the tenth and final mortal Sikh Guru, Guru Gobind Singh, when he created the Khalsa *panth* (order) in 1699. The Khalsa is the order of Sikhs who have formally pledged to live in accordance with the institutionalized Sikh code of conduct known as *rahit*. The creation of the Khalsa is widely considered by Sikhs as the final step in the codification of the Sikh way of life.

There is significant historiographical disagreement on whether the five Ks were really instituted by Guru Gobind Singh.[41] My contribution as a philosopher is not to sort out this complex historiography but rather to attempt to bring some philosophical clarity to questions about the role and significance of the five Ks. However, this historiography is still important to mention. For one thing, those who claim that the five Ks are a later development also tend to infer that this makes them discontinuous with the philosophy of SGGS itself. In this way, a central component of Sikh practice is presented as a kind of add-on, part of a nineteenth-century philosophical transformation of Sikh thought and practice. But this inference is not justified. Whether the five Ks were truly instituted by Guru Gobind Singh in 1699 does not settle whether their distinctively ethical significance in Sikh practice is continuous with the Sikh ethical theory espoused in SGGS.

On my interpretation, the ethical significance of the five Ks is as *commitments* to living in accordance with the Sikh ethical theory espoused in SGGS. Community understanding of the significance of each of the five Ks is already conducive to this interpretation. My contribution is to draw out the philosophical connections to the Sikh ethical theory. Of course, for many Sikhs, the significance of the five Ks is highly personal, so I cannot hope to provide an interpretation that captures every aspect of this significance for everyone. Nevertheless, I think my interpretation is helpful for understanding the place of the five Ks in Sikh ethics.

This interpretation is meant to capture several related thoughts that are uncontroversial in the community understanding of the general significance of the five Ks. One such thought, expressed by many who bear the five Ks, is that these articles (*bānā*) are an outward reflection of the philosophical teachings they follow (*bānī*). Another is that the visible form (*rūp*) of those who carry the five Ks identifies them publicly as following a certain set of values, and dependable to uphold those values. Finally, there is the idea that the five Ks, as physical objects placed on the body, serve as corporeal reminders, with physical weight, of the weight of one's commitment to Sikh values.

Two questions remain. First, what commitments do each of the five Ks represent? Second, how are these commitments related to the Sikh ethical theory? Here my contribution is most novel, as I take the answer to the first question to be guided by the answer to the second.

---

[41] For skepticism, see Pashaura Singh (1999) and McLeod (2003, 2007). For defense of the communal narrative, see Grewal (2010) and Bhupinder Singh (2014). For further discussion of historical sources, see Malhotra (2014).

5.1.1 Kes

Kes is undoubtedly the most significant of the five Ks, and the most definitive of what it is to be an observant Sikh. Keeping *kes* involves refraining from cutting the hair on one's head and from shaving one's facial hair. Sikh men who keep *kes* generally keep their hair tied up and covered with a *dastār* (Sikh turban), giving them a distinctive appearance. The *dastār* is less commonly worn by Sikh women, who generally keep their uncut hair in a braid or bun, covered with a *chunni* (headscarf), but in some Sikh communities, wearing the *dastār* is standard for women and men alike.

If each of the five Ks represents a commitment, what commitment does *kes* represent? One commonly expressed thought is that *kes* represents a commitment to respecting our natural form, as the Divine created us, rather than altering that form. However, this picture faces significant difficulties. For one thing, it is not clear why refraining from altering our natural physical form would be important. While we have been in a sense "created" with this form by the Divine, we have also been "created" with the natural condition of *haumai*. And yet, *haumai* is something to be subdued, and so one aspect of our natural condition is to be altered. Thus, it cannot be that the bare fact of being part of our natural condition is ethically significant. For another, this justification for keeping *kes* inevitably devolves into inane questions of where to draw the line, such as why Sikhs still trim their fingernails, even though this alters their natural form.

Another thought has to do with the significance of the *dastār*. Sikhs will often describe the *dastār* as the crown of a king, given to all Sikhs by Guru Gobind Singh to show that all are equal. The emphasis on equality is definitely on the right track, but this does not directly attribute any significance to *kes* itself, only to the *dastār*. A Sikh who wore a *dastār* on top of cut hair would not thereby keep *kes*, so this cannot quite be correct either.

But there is something right in both of these thoughts. I suggest that the significance of *kes* does have to do with a commitment to the natural order, but a more specific one. What the natural growth of *kes* represents, more specifically, is a commitment to living in accordance with *hukam* – the natural order of interrelation between all things and the Divine. If the meaning of *kes* is interpreted in this way, then its ethical significance is no mystery. Recall the passage discussed in Section 2:

ਕਿਵ ਸਚਿਆਰਾ ਹੋਈਐ ਕਿਵ ਕੂੜੈ ਤੁਟੈ ਪਾਲਿ ॥
Kiv sachiārā hoīai kiv kūrhai ṯutai pāl.
How can one become a truthful person? How can the veil of falsehood be torn away?

ਹੁਕਮਿ ਰਜਾਈ ਚਲਣਾ ਨਾਨਕ ਲਿਖਿਆ ਨਾਲਿ ॥੧॥
Hukam rajāī chalṇā Nānak likhiā nāl. ||1||
By walking in accordance with *hukam*, Nanak, so it is written. ||1|| (1)

If *kes* is the outward reflection of a commitment to walking in accordance with *hukam*, then it represents the most general commitment one can make to following Sikh ethics: to be true the ultimate reality of Oneness.

This also explains what *kes* has to do with equality. As discussed in the previous section, truthful living involves treating all with equality and eschewing social hierarchies. If *kes* represents a general commitment to being truthful to ultimate reality, this includes a commitment to equality. This explanation of the significance of *kes* (and by extension, *dastār*) fits with the idea that it is an outward expression of the *gurū*'s teachings. It also fits with the ideas that it makes one answerable publicly for upholding one's values, and that it serves as a physical reminder of the weight of one's commitment. Finally, this way of understanding the significance of *kes* in Sikh practice makes sense of why *kes* is the most important of the five Ks: it is the most important because it is an outward reflection of the most general commitment to following the Sikh ethic of truthful living.

5.1.2 Kanghā

The *kanghā* is a small wooden comb, which is not only used to comb the hair but also tucked into the hair to keep it tied up. Academic discussions of the significance of the *kanghā* almost always connect it to the rejection of ascetic self-denial in Sikh thought. Recounting Kapur Singh's (1959) interpretation of the five Ks, Bhupinder Singh writes that the *kangha* is "an obvious complement to unshorn hair, is an injunction against matted hair or dreadlocks symbolising asceticism and renunciation of the world" (2014, 131). Similarly, N.G.K. Singh writes that the function of the *kanghā* is "to keep [one's hair] tidy, in contrast with the recluses who kept it matted as a token of their having renounced the world" (2011, 51). While this is correct, it must be added that the *kangha* is not just a symbol but the outward reflection of a commitment.

Recall this line from SGGS, quoted in the previous section:

ਜਟਾ ਧਾਰਿ ਧਾਰਿ ਜੋਗੀ ਮੂਏ ਤੇਰੀ ਗਤਿ ਇਨਹਿ ਨ ਪਾਈ ॥੨॥
Jatā dhār dhār jogī mūe terī gat ineh na pāī. ||2||
The Yogis die with matted hair; even then, they do not find Your nature. ||2|| (654)

Here we can see that, matted hair is used to represent the misguidedness of ascetic self-denial in Sikh ethics. Now recall another line discussed in the previous section:

ਕਹੁ ਨਾਨਕ ਗੁਰੁ ਪੂਰਾ ਭੇਟਿਆ ਪਰਵਾਣੁ ਗਿਰਸਤ ਉਦਾਸ ॥੪॥੪॥੫॥

Kaho Nānak gur pūrā bheṭiā parvāṇ girsat udās. ||4||4||5||

Says Nanak, one who meets the perfect *gurū* is both householder and
  renunciate. ||4||4||5|| (496)

Sikh ethics enjoins one to be both householder and renunciate: a person who lives in the world of ordinary experiences while also renouncing the false duality that structures it. Thus, the *kangha* can be seen as the outward reflection of a commitment to living in this way. This illuminates how *kangha* is related to *kes*. The *kangha* represents a commitment to practicing Oneness without renouncing the world. By keeping one's *kes* combed and tidy, one prevents one's general commitment to truthful living (represented by *kes*) from being transformed into a self-indulgent renunciation of the world (represented by matted hair).

In this way, *kangha* can be seen as having ethical significance that is auxiliary to that of *kes*. While it is not necessarily outwardly visible, it makes up a part of the overall form (*rūp*) one presents to the world, and thus one's answerability, both to oneself and others, for living up to one's commitments.

5.1.3 Kaṛā

The *kaṛā* is a steel bracelet worn on the wrist of the dominant hand. It has been ascribed a variety of meanings by Sikhs, but the most common is that the *kaṛā*, being felt always when one moves one's dominant hand, is a constant reminder to be aware of what one does by one's own hand. In this way, it can be seen as the outward reflection of the commitment not to let oneself be ruled by one's appetites, and to always exercise self-control. Thus, it is closely related to the virtue of *sanjam* discussed in Section 3. To have *sanjam* is to be the master of one's appetites, rather than the other way around. By reminding one to always be in control of one actions, the *kaṛā* represents and reminds the Sikh of their commitment to self-control.

The ethical significance of the *kaṛā* can also be connected to the virtue of *bibek* (discernment). Though she does not draw this connection explicitly, it is evoked by N.G.K. Singh (2011) in a brief discussion of the significance of the *kaṛā*, where she quotes the following line from SGGS:

ਕਰ ਕਰਿ ਕਰਤਾ ਕੰਗਨ ਪਹਿਰੈ ਇਨ ਬਿਧਿ ਚਿਤੁ ਧਰੇਈ ॥੨॥

Kar kar kartā kangan pahirai in bidh chit dhareī. ||2||

She who wears the bracelet of the Divine around her wrist shall hold her con-
  sciousness steady. ||2| (359)

The importance of a steady consciousness in Sikh ethics is captured by the virtue of *bibek*. As discussed in Section 3, *bibek* is necessary for subduing *haumai*, because it is the virtue that allows one to discern when one is acting out of *haumai*. The *kaṛā*, insofar as it functions as a reminder to be aware of, and thus reflect on, one's own actions, can be related to *bibek* in addition to *sanjam*.

More generally, the *kaṛā*, with its weight on one's arm, seems to represent a commitment to ensuring that one does not act out of *haumai*. Given that *haumai* is the condition of our existence, such a commitment is clearly one of which we would need constant reminding. As an outward reflection of this commitment, the *kaṛā* makes Sikhs answerable, both to themselves and others, for living up to their commitment to ensure they do not act out of *haumai*. In this way, the ethical significance of the *kaṛā* is clearly continuous with the ethical theory presented in SGGS.

5.1.4 Kachherā

Kachherā are an undergarment similar to boxer shorts. Like the *kaṛā*, *kachherā* are often connected to ideas of self-control and restraining one's appetites. Given their proximity to the sexual organs, *kachherā* are seen as especially representative of the importance of controlling or restraining one's sexual desire, and thus to avoiding the vice of *kām*. While there is something to this, I think there is a more general commitment represented by *kachherā*, which can be drawn out by focusing on the fact that it is an undergarment and thus not generally visible, unlike the *kaṛā*.

I have connected the *kaṛā* to self-control over one's appetites. Because excessive appetites, as a manifestation of *haumai*, are a fact of life, the virtue of *sanjam* or self-control is of great importance. But, as previously discussed, it is also of great importance to attempt to prevent one's appetites from multiplying in this way in the first place. This is where the virtue of *santokh* (contentment) comes in. While *sanjam* is the virtue of controlling the appetites one has, *santokh* is the virtue of limiting the growth of one's appetites in the first place. In this way, *santokh* operates as a check on the influence of *haumai* at an earlier stage than *sanjam* does. For example, to avoid the vice of *kām* requires not just that one refrain from acting out of objectifying lust but also that one refrain from having the objectifying thoughts and feelings that would give rise to such action. This requires not just *sanjam* but also *santokh*.

Now return to the comparison between *kaṛā* and *kachherā*. While the *kaṛā*, always visible on one's wrist, is the most outward and public reflection of one's commitment to subduing *haumai*, the *kachherā* are the most inward and private reflection of this commitment, only visible in intimate settings. What I suggest we take from this is that, as the *kaṛā* is related to *sanjam*, the *kachherā* are related to *santokh*. That is, while the *kaṛā* represents in the first instance one's commitment to controlling one's appetites, the *kachherā* represent in the first instance one's commitment to preventing these appetites from growing and multiplying. Thus, as an undergarment, the *kachherā* represent what is in some ways the most private virtue – one that operates much earlier in the explanation of one's conduct – not at the stage of action but at the stage of thought and feeling.

5.1.5 Kirpān *(and a Note on Justice)*

The *kirpān* is in many ways the most difficult of the five Ks to connect to the ethical theory presented in SGGS. This is because the *kirpān* is the only one of the five Ks that is a weapon. As such, it seems much more obviously connected to the martial direction of Sikhism under the later *gurūs* than it does to the message of SGGS. However, Guru Gobind Singh clearly saw the martial direction of Sikh practice, as begun by Guru Hargobind, with its ideal of the *sant sipāhī* (saint-soldier), as continuous with the philosophy of SGGS. In order to connect the *kirpan* to the Sikh ethical theory, we must return to a virtue I set aside in Section 3: justice.

As a reminder, I set justice (*niāo*) aside because its role in SGGS is not analogous to that of the virtues discussed in Section 3. *Niāo* is referenced many times in SGGS, but it is not usually ascribed to humans as a character trait along with other virtues. Instead, *niāo* is largely referenced in association with the Divine:

ਏਕਾ ਮੂਰਤਿ ਸਾਚਾ ਨਾਉ ॥
Ekā mūrat sāchā nāo.
Ultimate reality is One, the True Name.

ਤਿਥੈ ਨਿਬੜੈ ਸਾਚੁ ਨਿਆਉ ॥
Tithai nibṛai sāch niāo.
There, true justice is determined.

ਸਾਚੀ ਕਰਣੀ ਪਤਿ ਪਰਵਾਣੁ ॥
Sāchī karṇī pat parvāṇ.
The practice of truth is honored and accepted.

ਸਾਚੀ ਦਰਗਹ ਪਾਵੈ ਮਾਣੁ ॥੬॥
Sāchī ḍargeh pāvai māṇ. ||6||
The truthful are honored in the realm of ultimate reality. ||6|| (1188)

This passage sheds light on justice (*niāo*) in two ways. First, justice is said to be determined from the vantage point of ultimate reality. Second, the determination of justice is connected to honoring and accepting the practice of truth, which connects justice to truthful living in general.

I contend that justice is not meant to be a particular virtue, in the sense of a particular aspect of truthfulness. Instead, like wisdom, justice seems more like a particular *guise* of truthfulness. The truthful person practices truth, and true justice is determined to be nothing but the practice of truth. But then what is the point of understanding truthful living under the guise of justice? The answer seems to lie in the fact that, at the level of ultimate reality, all social hierarchies and divisions vanish. Recall the discussion of *dharam* from the previous section. SGGS lays out a stringent moral obligation to treat everyone with equality, and to reject caste and other social hierarchies. This, I think, has always been the Sikh conception of justice: truthful living under the guise of fighting for the equal standing of all.

Almost all of SGGS was compiled by the fifth Sikh *gurū*, Guru Arjan Dev as the Adi Granth. At that point, Sikhs had lived relatively peacefully within the Mughal Empire, which had been mostly religiously tolerant. That changed when the emperor Jehangir ordered the execution of Guru Arjan Dev. The historical scholarship on this event is fraught, but it is widely agreed that the execution was at least partly motivated by the increasing prominence of the Sikh movement, which Jehangir saw as a threat.[42] According to Sikh communal history, before his execution, Guru Arjan Dev instructed his son and successor, Guru Hargobind, to take up arms and resist persecution. This is seen as a crucial turning point in the relationship between Sikh thought and ethical practice, at which it became clear that Sikhs would not be left in peace to pursue their way of life. Instead, martial and political organization was necessary to combat injustice.

Because the ethical theory laid out in SGGS was already basically complete, this increasingly explicit focus on justice as a virtue is not present in SGGS. But the political reality laid bare a central truth already contained in that theory: if Sikhs are serious about practicing Oneness, then they cannot acquiesce to the injustices of religious persecution. Moreover, it becomes clear that, whether it was done to them or to others, injustice to anyone could not be countenanced as part of a commitment to practicing Oneness. If all are One, then injustice anywhere is a threat to justice everywhere. This thought is embodied in the decision of the ninth Sikh *gurū*, Guru Tegh Bahadur, to subject himself to

---

[42] For more on this issue, see Pashaura Singh (2005).

martyrdom in the course of attempting to protect other oppressed groups from persecution.

Though this more political understanding of justice is less explicitly emphasized in SGGS, it is a direct extension of the ethics presented therein. The injunction to fight against injustice wherever it is found can be derived straightforwardly from the injunction to look upon all with equality, combined with the existence of manifestly unjust political and social conditions. Moreover, SGGS does criticize unjust political authorities and institutions, even when the language of justice (*niāo*) is not explicitly used.[43] Finally, it must not be overlooked that SGGS harshly condemns unjust social practices such as the caste system and *satī* (widow-burning). Thus, though it was a result of increasing martial and political organization, the more explicit emphasis on justice as a virtue for Sikhs is fully continuous with the message of SGGS.

This brings me back, finally, to the ethical significance of the *kirpān*. The *kirpān* is widely understood by Sikhs to be the outward reflection of a commitment to justice. Moreover, the commitment to justice is thought to be manifested by a sword precisely in light of the realization that justice must be fought for. Though the *kirpān* is less often carried by present-day Sikhs as a functional weapon, it was originally meant to be a real means of standing up for justice, to be wielded in self-defense or in defense of others (but never in aggression). Whether it is worn as a functional weapon or not, the *kirpān* for Sikhs represents a commitment to standing up not just for oneself but for those who are unable to stand up for themselves. Moreover, Sikhs who carry the *kirpān* are answerable both to themselves and to others for living up to this commitment.

In this way, the ethical significance of the *kirpān* is unified with that of the other *kakār*. All of the five Ks, I have argued, are outward physical reflections of inner ethical commitments. Moreover, these ethical commitments are completely continuous and coherent with the ethical theory presented in SGGS. Before moving on, however, a clarification is important. As outward reflections of inner ethical commitments, the five Ks reinforce these commitments by constantly reminding the wearer of them, as well as adding a layer of answerability for living up to them. But this by no means implies that only those who wear the five Ks live up to these commitments (or even sincerely make them). Though the five Ks have great significance in Sikh ethical practice, wearing the

---

[43] Guru Nanak criticized Mughal rulers in several *sabads*. For example, he stridently criticizes government officials for abusing and extorting the public (SGGS 1288). A similar *sabad* of Guru Arjan (SGGS 1356) criticizes rulers for their cruelty and oppression. Though these *sabads* do not explicitly invoke *niāo* or any other term for justice, they clearly show that the Sikh Gurus were concerned about political injustice from the beginning.

five Ks is neither necessary nor sufficient for being a good Sikh. Indeed, a person who practices Oneness without keeping the five Ks would be a better person than one who wears the five Ks but constantly acts out of *haumai*. Moreover, it could be seen as a kind of dishonesty or hypocrisy to wear the five Ks without having a sincere commitment to practicing Oneness.

5.2 The Three Pillars

In the communal understanding of Sikh ethics, Sikhs are enjoined to live according to three pillars of conduct: *nām japnā* (meditate on the Divine name), *kirat karnī* (earn an honest living), and *vaṇḍ chhaknā* (share what one has). Scholars attribute these three pillars to a 1907 novel of Bhai Vir Singh, where they are thought to be inspired by the three pillars of conduct that appear in SGGS as *nām dān isnān*.[44] As discussed in the previous section, *nām* refers to contemplation of the Divine Name, which takes the form of scriptural recitation and devotional singing. *Dān* refers to beneficence (especially the sharing of resources), and *isnān* refers to purity of conduct. Though this connection between scripture and practice has long been drawn, my goal here is to present it in a systematic form.

5.2.1 Nām japnā

The relationship between *nām* in *nām dān isnān* and the pillar of *nām japnā* is obvious. *Nām japnā* is the more contemplative aspect of the practice of Oneness. It is meditation on the Divine Name. Recall what is said in the *mūl mantar* (root verse) of SGGS: the name of the Divine – the One (*ik oaṅkār*) – is Truth. Thus, to meditate on the Divine Name is to meditate on the fundamental truth of the Oneness of all existence. To live truthfully, one must contemplate this truth, understand it, and take it to heart.

Moreover, there is a mystical component to *nām japnā*. By meditating on the Divine Name, one is thought to achieve a kind of temporary attunement and direct access to ultimate reality. For example, through repeated chanting of the phrase *vāhigurū satnām* (wonderous Guide, whose name is Truth), it is thought that one can achieve a kind of consonance between the vibration of one's utterances and the One cosmic vibration (*ik oaṅkār*).[45] Because Oneness is the foundation of all ethical truths, *nām japnā* can be seen as enabling a kind of direct access to these ethical truths. Thus, while the role of *nām japnā* in

---

[44] This connection was first drawn in 1927 by Puran Singh (see his 1976 book). See Dewan Singh (1973) and Nirvikar Singh (2019) for further discussion.

[45] For a detailed exposition of the ethical and metaphysical significance of sound, rhythm, and vibration in Sikh thought, see Kaur (2025).

practicing Oneness can be seen as in part epistemic, it is not purely intellectual or cognitive.

The ethical significance of *nām japnā* also goes beyond its epistemic role in attaining access to the Divine. *Nām japnā* is also seen as central to achieving *sahaj*. As discussed in the previous section, *sahaj* is the mode of consciousness in which one is able to see through duality to the Oneness of all. Part of the role of *nām japnā* is to effect a kind of centering – a quieting of the chaos of the individuated self. By meditating on the Divine Name, one can put oneself in a position to structure one's agency through Oneness rather than self-other duality. In this way, the role of *nām japnā* in practicing Oneness is not just epistemic but also practical.

5.2.2 Kirat karnī

Kirat karnī means roughly, to earn an honest living. Recall that the theory of right conduct in SGGS enjoins one to be a householder, but to engage in worldly pursuits within the *gurū*'s wisdom. If one is to be a householder, it cannot be that all accumulation of resources such as wealth and property is prohibited. Ordinary personal pursuits, such as a well-paying job that can support home-ownership and financial stability, are not seen as necessary incompatible with practicing Oneness. But the qualifier "within the *gurū*'s wisdom" places signifi-cant limitations on such pursuits. These are the limitations referred to in *kirat karnī*'s enjoinder to earn an *honest* living. In the original three pillars of *nām dān isnān*, *kirat karnī* is therefore an extension of *isnān*.

As discussed in the previous section, *isnān* (purity) refers to refraining from conduct that pollutes one's consciousness with *haumai*. *Isnān* thus picks out negative duties: constraints on what we may permissibly do. *Kirat karnī* says that it is permissible to earn a living but that this is constrained by what is honest. Clearly, this rules out certain methods of accumulation of resources that plainly go against the principles of Sikh ethics. This includes actions that manifest *lobh* (greed), as well as any other methods that manifest *haumai*, including deception, coercion, and exploitation. These are already significant constraints on the permissible accumulation of resources.

Is there anything more specific to be gleaned from Sikh ethics about earning an honest living? To answer this question, we can further examine the fact that some accumulation of resources is taken to be compatible with practicing Oneness. Here, an important implication of Sikh ethics becomes clear: whatever is compatible with *my* practicing Oneness must be compatible with anyone else's doing the same. The practice of Oneness is, by its nature, constrained by a kind of universalizability. This is because a nonuniversalizable practice would necessarily involve making an exception of oneself, and thereby according to oneself a significance one denies to others. But this is just to act out of *haumai*. So the practice of Oneness cannot be nonuniversalizable.

The above entails that whatever accumulation of resources is compatible with practicing Oneness cannot be incompatible with a similar accumulation of resources by others. This builds on the discussion of the significant limits placed by the theory of right conduct in SGGS on the accumulation of resources. Whatever one accumulates for oneself cannot constitute the earning of an honest living if it is at the expense of others' ability to earn an honest living. Though this principle is compatible with a certain amount of inequality in wealth and property, it also places significant limits on this inequality. Indeed, it is difficult to see how the hoarding of vast capital can be compatible with the pillar of *kirat karnī*, given the vast suffering and exploitation on which it depends. Indeed, *kirat karnī* can be understood not just as placing limits on how one may personally pursue the accumulation of resources but on what kind of social system one may support and benefit from. For example, it is difficult to reconcile *kirat karnī* with support for our global economic system and the massive disparities it maintains.

5.2.3 Vaṇḍ chhaknā

Vaṇḍ chhaknā means roughly to share what one has. Just as *dān* picks out positive duties of beneficence as the flipside to the negative duties picked out by *isnān*, so *vaṇḍ chhaknā* can be seen as the flipside of *kirat karnī*. While *kirat karnī* places constraints on the accumulation of resources such as wealth and property, *vaṇḍ chhaknā* shows that this is not sufficient for right conduct. While it is true that the practice of Oneness is compatible with some accumulation of resources, there is a sense in which these things should not be seen as truly and deeply one's own. To see them this way would be to mistake the surface level individuation of selves for a deep division in ultimate reality, and thus to enforce the shallow self-other duality of ordinary empirical existence.

Just as *haumai* involves the repeated assertion of the ego, "I am me," so too it involves the repeated assertion of possession, "this is mine." To be too attached to one's own possessions is the vice of *moh*. The addition of *vaṇḍ chhaknā* to *kirat karnī* suggests that even that which has been earned honestly must not be held with too much attachment, lest one mistake the shallow truth of "this is mine" for some deep reality. This is why, in order to practice Oneness, we must generously share what we have with others, rather than hoarding it protectively.

Vaṇḍ chhaknā is often practiced through donating a significant amount of one's income to charity. But the use of the term "charity" here should not give the impression that this is a mere recommendation. It is uncontroversial in Sikh ethical practice that donating a portion of one's wealth is an ethical *requirement*. The standard interpretation of this requirement is the *dasvandh*, which refers to the one-tenth of one's income one must donate to charity. However, the *dasvandh* should arguably be seen only as the bare minimum that everyone who is not in dire circumstances is able to reasonably give. For those of much more means, much more is arguably required in order to practice *vaṇ chhaknā*.

Of course, one might also take from the Sikh ethical theory that no one should be able to accumulate vast wealth in the first place. But given that this can easily happen in the actual world, charitable obligations may significantly exceed *dasvandh* for many. Moreover, as with *kirat karnī*, *vaṇ chhaknā* might be extended to a political principle in addition to a principle of individual conduct (e.g., to pay progressive taxes to fund social programs).

Aside from donating to charity, another important aspect of *vaṇ chhaknā* is the Sikh ethical practice of *seva*, or selfless service. In addition to wealth, another resource that is unequally distributed is *time*. According to Sikh ethical practice, one is required to share not only one's wealth but also one's time with others. This most often takes the form of volunteer work. A particularly striking example is that of Khalsa Aid, a Sikh humanitarian NGO devoted to providing support to victims of both natural and manmade disasters across the globe. But it also takes the form of simple acts of kindness and beneficence on an everyday basis, done without any reward or compensation.

Importantly, *seva* has not just a practical role to play in enacting Oneness but also an epistemic role. By practicing truly selfless service, one elides the boundary between self and other. According to Sikh communal thought, this creates an experience of transcendence of self-other duality. Such an experience constitutes another form of attunement and direct access to ultimate reality. In other words, this experience of treating oneself and another as One is an experience of the Divine.

This sheds further light on how there is no real separation between the epistemic attainment of truth and the practice of truth, just as there is no real separation between metaphysics and ethics in Sikh philosophy. Understanding and practicing Oneness are inextricably linked. As we have already seen, the full experience of the Divine requires both understanding and practice together and can only be achieved through doing good deeds for others, not just through solitary contemplation. This ties back in with why renunciation of the world is rejected as a pathway to experiencing the Divine in SGGS. Moreover, it shows how *nām japnā* is more closely related to *vaṇ chhaknā* and *kirat karnī* than it might initially seem to be. As with the original *nām dān isnān*, each of the three pillars of conduct is an important aspect of truthful living, and all must be integrated into a holistic practice of Oneness that suffuses thought, feeling, and action.

5.3 Kīrtan and Langar

Finally, an explanation of the relationship between Sikh ethical theory and practice is incomplete without a discussion of *sabad kirtan* (collective singing) and *langar* (communal dining). Thus far, I have only mentioned these practices in passing. Though the initial development of both practices was contemporaneous with SGGS, they have evolved to become deeply institutionalized facets of Sikh practice. In discussing the ethical significance of *sabad kīrtan* and *langar*, I attempt to show how the development of these practices is, like that of other significant Sikh ethical practices, an application of the ethical theory presented in SGGS.

My discussion here builds on that of Inderjit Kaur, who argues that the pairing of *sabad kīrtan* and *langar* constitutes an "everyday practice of non-Othering" (2024, 229).

As emphasized by Kaur, the practice of non-Othering is an essential aspect of the practice of Oneness. She analyzes Othering as "a fundamentally divisive and hierarchical process of constructing social groups as we/us versus they/them, where the Other is posited as inferior and even threatening" (231). Kaur's analysis makes clear how the process of Othering reflects an attachment to self-other duality. As such, Othering is essentially a manifestation of *haumai*.

Both *sabad kīrtan* and *langar* take place in the *gurdwarā* – the Sikh place of worship (lit. doorway to the *gurū*), and together make up the most central parts of the Sikh service. The site of the *gurdwarā* is meant to be an essentially inclusive and egalitarian one. It is a space open to all, regardless of religion, caste, race, gender, etc.[46] Furthermore, the inclusivity of this space is meant to reflect the nonexistence of social hierarchies in the Court of the Divine – that is, at the level of ultimate reality. Upon entering the *gurdwarā*, one is to leave all of these dualities at the *gurū*'s doorway before stepping into the space of Oneness.

Once in the *gurdwarā*, devotional practices are structured so as to reflect a commitment to egalitarianism. In both the *divān* hall, where *sabad kīrtan* is sung, and the *langar* hall, everyone sits on the floor together regardless of social positionality, which reflects the equal worth of all people and reinforces a lack of hierarchy. This feature of *sabad kīrtan* and *langar* was quite radical in the social context in which these practices were developed. The practice of the caste

---

[46] At least, it is supposed to be. As with any religious practice, things can go awry, as in the existence of caste-specific *gurdware*. These are completely incompatible with Sikh ethics and cannot be understood as anything but a perversion of Sikh ethical practices.

system forbade people of high caste from mingling with those of low caste and considered the former polluted if they did. Moreover, it was considered proper for ordinary people to sit on the floor, while rulers and aristocrats sat elevated on thrones and the like. This makes particularly clear how everyone sitting on the floor together is supposed to reflect and reinforce egalitarianism and the rejection of social hierarchies.

As mentioned earlier, *nām japnā* – meditation on the Divine Name – is supposed to facilitate a kind of direct experience of the ultimate reality of Oneness, and correspondingly enable one to enter *sahaj* – the mode of consciousness that eschews self-other duality, from which one is capable of practicing Oneness. Building on Kaur's analysis, we might think of *sahaj as* the *non-Othering* mode of consciousness. Though *nām japnā* can be practiced through solitary meditation or chanting, *sabad kīrtan* is the primary form of *nām japnā* practiced in the social site of the *gurdwārā*. As an essentially social practice of collective *nām japnā, sabad kīrtan* is thus thought to enable a correspondingly collective experience of Oneness. In engaging in this collective spiritual activity, each individual is (ideally) able to temporarily forget their individuated self and so experience the lack of distinction between themselves and the other participants.

While *sabad kīrtan* relates most closely to the pillar of *nām japnā*, the practice of *langar* relates more closely to the pillars of *kirat karnī* and *vaṇḍ chhaknā*. The *langar* hall is open to all, whether they are Sikhs are not, to dine communally. No one is ever charged for dining there. In addition to sitting communally on the floor, everyone is served the same simple, vegetarian food. As Kaur emphasizes, all of these features of *langar* are aspects of creating an egalitarian space free of Othering. Additionally, the practice of *langar* is defined not just by the lack of Othering but by the positive practice of Oneness through serving as a community kitchen that exists for the benefit of all people.

In its function as a community kitchen, *langar* is one of the most important forms of *sevā* (selfless service) in Sikh ethical practice. As I have emphasized, *sevā* is an essential practice for Sikhs, seen as necessary for fully recognizing the Oneness of all and reflecting it in one's conduct. The experience of acting for the sake of others also constitutes another form of direct experience of the ultimate reality of Oneness. In this way, the practices of *sabad kīrtan* and *langar* are unified as the institutionalized practice of Oneness. Together, they constitute the *gurdwārā* as a site of Oneness and a refuge from the unjust social hierarchies that structure the world of individuated selves. In this way, *sabad kīrtan* and *langar* are not only continuous with the three pillars of conduct but also directly continuous with the ethic of truthful living presented in SGGS.

5.4 Conclusion

I have presented an interpretation of a variety of Sikh ethical practices on which they are continuous with the ethical theory presented in SGGS. According to this theory, the ethical life is about truthful living – living in a way that is true to the ultimate Oneness of all and the shallowness of self-other duality. I have argued that for all of the most central Sikh ethical practices, the communal understanding of these practices connects them clearly to truthful living in the form of the practice of Oneness.

Much of what I have argued for will not be very surprising to practicing Sikhs (though some of my interpretation is novel, and hopefully its systematic presentation will be illuminating even for them). However, my interpretation goes against a significant thread in the academic literature on these practices, where some scholars have claimed that a variety of Sikh ethical practices are modern inventions created by reform movements in an effort to further distinguish Sikhs from other religious groups.

One thing I hope to have shown here is that such claims face a serious challenge: if Sikh practices are the result of modern reforms, then why are they so clearly and deeply continuous with the ethical theory presented in SGGS? Such claims have already been scrutinized for paying insufficient attention to Sikh communal history, as well as counterevidence in the historical record. But they also pay insufficient attention to the philosophical threads running through text and practice. Etiological and historiographical disputes aside, Sikhs' own communal understanding of their ethical practices and institutions as applications and extensions of the ethical theory of SGGS has been basically correct, despite claims to the contrary.

Concluding Remarks

In this Element, I have presented an interpretation of the Sikh ethical theory, drawn out from close engagement with the text of Sri Guru Granth Sahib, proceeding from the assumption that it contains a coherent and systematic theory. On my interpretation, the cornerstone of Sikh ethics (and indeed, the cornerstone of all Sikh philosophy) is truth (*sat/sach*). In SGGS, the *mūl mantar* – root verse – identifies the Divine with the fundamental metaphysical truth, the ultimate reality of Oneness. Thus, Sikh ethics and metaphysics are unified: ethics is fundamentally about living in a way that is true to the ultimate reality of Oneness.

I have explained how various components of the Sikh ethical theory flow from this conception of the ethical life as the truthful life. One component is the Sikh account of the unity of vices and virtues. The fundamental source of vice is *haumai*, the attachment to self-other duality. It unifies the "five thieves" *kām* (lust), *krodh* (wrath), *lobh* (greed), *moh* (attachment), and *ahankār* (arrogance). The fundamental virtue is truthfulness, the virtue of the *sachiārā*. It unifies particular virtues such as *daiā* (compassion), *santokh* (contentment), *sanjam* (self-control), *saram* (humility), and *bibek* (discernment). All of these virtues are aspects of truthfulness. Moreover, wisdom and justice can each be understood as fully general virtues that are guises of truthfulness.

Another component is the Sikh understanding of right conduct as truthful living (*sach āchār*). Truthful living is the practice of Oneness. Right conduct consists in action, thought, and feeling that are structured by a recognition of and commitment to the Oneness of everyone, and the shallowness of self-other duality. This requires acting for the sake of others without regard for their separation from oneself in the world of ordinary experience. I have also argued that Sikh ethical practices, even those developed after the codification of SGGS, are extensions or applications of the ethical theory presented in SGGS. This challenges on philosophical grounds the already historically suspect view on which Sikh ethical practices are purely modern reforms.

In presenting all of this, I take myself to have proven the initial assumption that there is a coherent and systematic Sikh ethics present in SGGS. As I mentioned in the introduction, my concern is not directly with defending this theory or convincing the reader of its truth. My primary concern has been to remedy the serious problem I lamented at the outset: that in the work produced by Anglophone philosophers working in the analytic tradition, Sikh philosophy is completely ignored and erased. Even as other world philosophical traditions have gained a foothold in what has historically been an intellectually Eurocentric field, Sikh philosophy has remained totally absent.

I have tried to accomplish the delicate task of using the methodology of analytic philosophy to present the Sikh ethical theory, while also remaining true to its autochthonous features. My hope is that the existence of this Element will go some way toward giving Sikh philosophy a seat at the table, along with all the other increasingly recognized world philosophies. Moreover, I hope that it can be of use to Sikhs looking to understand their own heritage as an intellectually rich and rigorous philosophical tradition.

In presenting the Sikh ethical theory, this Element has not engaged in what is called *comparative* philosophy – work that puts into conversation philosophical ideas from different cultures and traditions to make philosophical progress. Instead, I have presented Sikh ethics almost entirely on its own terms, with only occasional reference to the theories of other cultures and traditions. This was a conscious choice to show that Sikh philosophy can stand on its own. But once this has been shown, it becomes clear that there is great potential for comparative philosophy that incorporates the Sikh perspective. This is work I hope to explore in the future. For example, it would be fruitful to explore similarities and differences between Sikh and Buddhist conceptions of Oneness. It would also be fruitful to compare and contrast conceptions of universality and equality in Sikh and Western ethics.

On the topic of universality and equality in Sikh and Western ethics, there is one comparative note I wish to make here. The dominant Western narrative in the history of ideas attributes the development of egalitarian philosophical principles to the Enlightenment period in Europe. Drawing attention to Sikh philosophy challenges this narrative. As my interpretation has shown, Sikh ethics has well-developed principles of universality and equality with systematic foundations.[47] Moreover, the development of these principles precedes the development of similar principles by European philosophers by some 100–200 years.

For example, there is significant affinity between Sikh ethics and Kantian ethics, though the underlying metaphysics differ considerably. Both systems hold that all people, in virtue of shared features, are of equal worth and deserve equal concern. Both systems hold that good deeds done selfishly are wholly lacking in virtue. And both systems prescribe conduct that is motivated by a regard for others that is universal and not parochial. Finally, both systems hold that it is deeply wrong to deny others the significance one accords oneself by treating them as mere objects.

Kant, however, was notoriously inept at drawing out the egalitarian implications of his own system, as is notable from his racist views.[48] The founding thinkers of Sikh ethics, by contrast, recognized the wrongness of such prejudices from the outset, by rejecting the caste system even though it was ubiquitously practiced at the time. The Sikh Gurus were radical thinkers who rejected many of the unjust social norms of their time in both theory and practice. Kant, and many other European Enlightenment philosophers, failed at this to various degrees. Even Mill, who was radical in his defense of gender equality, also defended British colonialism.

Thus, the Western narrative on which modern ethical progress is a European achievement is false. When this is laid bare, the erasure of Sikh ethics in Anglophone philosophy is even more regrettable. Not only does it problematically ignore an interesting and plausible ethical theory, but it also promulgates a false Eurocentric narrative about ethical progress. To put the point another

---

[47] Of course, this is not to assume that Sikhs necessarily live up to their principles better than anyone else does.

[48] On Kant's racism, see Mills (2005).

way: some of the reasons not to ignore Sikh ethics are epistemic. By ignoring a viable theoretical option, we fail to consider the full range of candidates for ethical truth. But other reasons not to ignore Sikh ethics are reasons of justice. It is unjust to fail to recognize the important contributions Sikh ethics has made to the global history of ideas, and to global ethical progress. This is all the more reason to stop erasing Sikh philosophy and give it a seat at the table. Doing so can only enrich our philosophical resources for addressing the ethical problems of the present and future.

References

Bal, G. K. (2017). Virtues (Sikhism). In *Sikhism*, ed. A.-P. S. Mandair. Netherlands: Springer, 460–463. https://doi.org/10.1007/978-94-024-0846-1_460.

Bommarito, N. (2020). *Seeing Clearly: A Buddhist Guide to Life*. New York: Oxford University Press.

Cherry, M. (2021). *The Case for Rage: Why Anger Is Essential to Anti-Racist Struggle*. New York, NY: Oxford University Press.

Frye, M. (1983). *The Politics of Reality: Essays in Feminist Theory*. Trumansburg, NY: The Crossing Press.

Ganeri, J. (2011). *The Lost Age of Reason: Philosophy in Early Modern India 1450–1700*. New York, NY: Oxford University Press.

Garfield, J. L. (2022). *Buddhist Ethics: A Philosophical Exploration*. New York, NY: Oxford University Press.

Grewal, J. S. (2010). W.H. McLeod and Sikh Studies. *Journal of Punjab Studies*, 17(1–2), 115–144.

Habermas, J. (1979). *Communication and the Evolution of Society*. Toronto: Beacon Press.

Kaur, I. N. (2024). Sabad Kīrtan, Langar, and the Affective Embodied Experience of Non-Othering in Sikh Practice. In *Music and Dance as Everyday South Asia*, eds. Sarah L. Morelli and Zoe C. Sherinian. New York, NY: Oxford University Press, 229–242.

Kaur, I. N. (2025). *Sensational Rhythms of the Ineffable: Ethical Affects in Sikh Sabad Kirtan*. Oxford University Press.

Kohli, S. S. (1974). *Sikh Ethics*. New Delhi: Munshiram Manoharlal.

Lakatos, I. (1970, January). History of Science and Its Rational Reconstructions. In *PSA: Proceedings of the Biennial Meeting of the Philosophy of Science Association* (Vol. 1970. Cambridge University Press, 91–136.

Malhotra, K. K. (2014). Religious Beliefs and Practices: Eighteenth Century Sikhs. In *The Punjab Revisited: Social Order, Economic Life, Cultural Articulation, Politics, and Partition (18th–20th Centuries): Essays in Honour of Dr Kirpal Singh*, ed. K. K. Malhotra. Patiala: Punjabi University, 68–107.

Mandair, A. P. S. (2023). *Sikh Philosophy: Exploring Gurmat Concepts in a Decolonizing World*. London: Bloomsbury.

McLeod, W. H. (1968). *Guru Nanak and the Sikh Religion*. Oxford: Oxford Clarendon Press.

McLeod, W. H. (2003). *Sikhs of the Khalsa: A History of the Khalsa Rahit*. New Delhi: Oxford University Press.

McLeod, W. H. (2007). *Essays in Sikh History, Tradition, and Society*. New Delhi: Oxford University Press.

Mills, C. (2005). Kant's *Untermenschen*. In *Andrew Valls, Race and Racism in Modern Philosophy*. Ithaca, NY: Cornell University Press, 169–93.

Nussbaum, M. (1995). Objectification. *Philosophy & Public Affairs*, *24*(4), 249–291.

Nussbaum, M. (2016). *Anger and Forgiveness: Resentment, Generosity, Justice*. New York, NY: Oxford University Press.

Schaffer, J. (2010). Monism: The Priority of the Whole. *Philosophical Review*, *119*(1), 31–76.

SikhiToTheMax. www.sikhitothemax.org/.

Singh, A. (1966). *Ethics of the Sikhs*. PhD dissertation, Punjabi University.

Singh, A. (1970). *Ethics of the Sikhs*. Patiala, Punjab: Punjabi University.

Singh, B. (2014). The Five Symbols of Sikhism: Some Contemporary Issues. *Sikh Formations*, *10*(1), 105–172.

Singh, D. (1973). *Mysticism of Guru Nanak*, PhD dissertation, Chandigarh: Panjab University.

Singh, D. (2001). Guru Nanak's Concept of Sahaj. In *Teachings of Guru Nanak Dev*, ed. T. Singh. Patiala: Punjabi University, 73–78.

Singh, H. (2011). *The Encyclopedia of Sikhism*. Patiala: Punjabi University. 3rd ed.

Singh, J. (2018). Lost in Translation? The Emergence of the Digital Guru Granth Sahib. *Sikh Formations*, *14*(3–4), 339–351.

Singh, K. (1959). *Prasharprasna, or the Baisakhi of Guru Gobind Singh*. Jalandhar: Hind.

Singh, K. (1991). *Guru Nanak's Life and Thought*. Amritsar, Punjab: Guru Nanak Dev University.

Singh, K. (2021). Vice and Virtue in Sikh Ethics. *The Monist*, *104*(3), 319–336.

Singh, K. (2024). Book Review: "Sikh Philosophy: Exploring Gurmat Concepts in a Decolonizing World": Arvind-Pal Singh Mandair. *Sikh Research Journal*, *8*(2), 56–60.

Singh, N. (2018). The Challenge of Translating the Guru Granth Sahib: An Illustration and Preliminary Reflections. *Sikh Research Journal*, *3*(1), 1–22.

Singh, N. (2019). The Three Pillars of Sikhism: A Note on Origins. *Sikh Research Journal*, *4*(1), 45–52.

Singh, N. G. K. (2007). Translating Sikh Scripture into English. *Sikh Formations*, *3*(1), 33–49.

Singh, N. G. K. (2011). *Sikhism*. London: IB Taurus.

Singh, N. G. K. [as Kaur, G.] (1981). *Physics and Metaphysics of the Guru Granth Sahib*. Sterling.

Singh, P. (1976). *Spirit of the Sikh, Part I*. Patiala: Punjabi University.

Singh, P. (1999). Formulation of the Convention of the Five Ks: A Focus on the Evolution of the Khalsa Rahit. *International Journal of Punjab Studies*, 6(2), 155–169.

Singh, P. (2005). Understanding the Martyrdom of Guru Arjan. *Journal of Punjab Studies*, *12*(1), 29–62.

Singh, P. (2014). Gurmat: The Teachings of the Gurus. In *The Oxford Handbook of Sikh Studies*. Oxford: Oxford University Press, 224–239. https://doi.org/10.1093/oxfordhb/9780199699308.013.051.

Singh, T. (2001a). Guru Nanak's Conception of Dharma – Perception of Truth. In *Teachings of Guru Nanak Dev*, ed. T. Singh. Patiala: Punjabi University, 3rd Ed, 10–19.

Singh, T. (2001b). Guru Nanak's Conception of Haumai (Ego). In *Teachings of Guru Nanak Dev*, ed. T. Singh. Patiala: Punjabi University, 3rd Ed, 30–38.

Sri Granth, a Sri Guru Granth Sahib search engine and resource. www.srigranth.org/.

Acknowledgments

I am grateful to Inderjit Kaur and Nirvikar Singh for many rounds of detailed feedback on drafts of this work. Without being able to consult their deep knowledge of both SGGS and scholarship on Sikh thought, this would have been an impossible undertaking. I am also grateful to two anonymous referees for helpful comments, as well as to Yujin Nagasawa for his patience and support as series editor.

Cambridge Elements≡

Global Philosophy of Religion

Yujin Nagasawa
University of Oklahoma

Yujin Nagasawa is Kingfisher College Chair of the Philosophy of Religion and Ethics and Professor of Philosophy at the University of Oklahoma. He is the author of *The Problem of Evil for Atheists* (2024), *Maximal God: A New Defence of Perfect Being Theism* (2018), *Miracles: A Very Short Introduction* (2018), *The Existence of God: A Philosophical Introduction* (2011), and *God and Phenomenal Consciousness* (2008), along with numerous articles. He is the editor-in-chief of *Religious Studies* and served as the president of the British Society for the Philosophy of Religion from 2017 to 2019.

About the Series

This Cambridge Elements series provides concise and structured overviews of a wide range of religious beliefs and practices, with an emphasis on global, multi-faith viewpoints. Leading scholars from diverse cultural backgrounds and geographical regions explore topics and issues that have been overlooked by Western philosophy of religion.

For EU product safety concerns, contact us at Calle de José Abascal, 56–1°,
28003 Madrid, Spain or eugpsr@cambridge.org.

www.ingramcontent.com/pod-product-compliance
Lightning Source LLC
LaVergne TN
LVHW010912030626
840340LV00033B/661